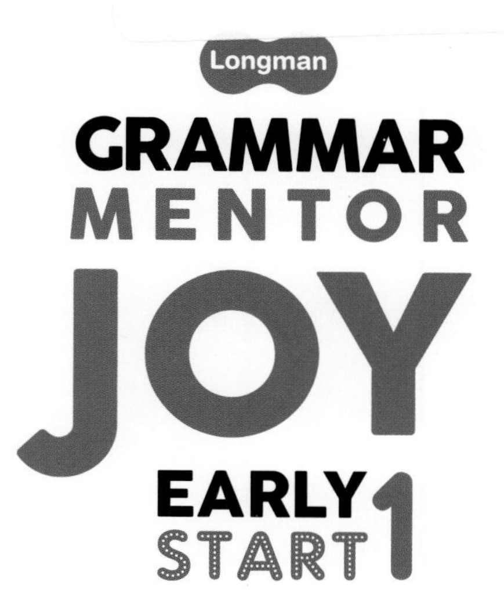
Longman
GRAMMAR
MENTOR
JOY
EARLY
START
1

Pearson

Longman
**GRAMMAR MENTOR JOY**
**EARLY START 1**

지은이 교재개발연구소
편집 및 기획 English Nine
발행처 Pearson Education South Asia Pte Ltd.
판매처 inkedu(inkbooks)
전화 02-455-9620(주문 및 고객지원)
팩스 02-455-9619
등록 제13-579호



ISBN 979-11-88228-28-7

# GRAMMAR MENTOR JOY

그래머
멘토
조이
얼리
스타트
하나

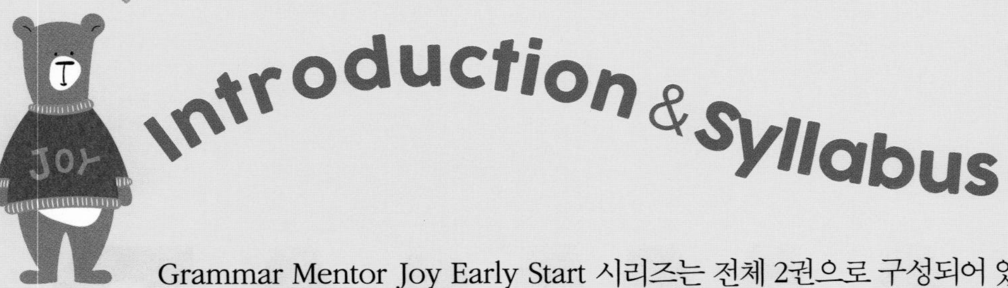


Grammar Mentor Joy Early Start 시리즈는 전체 2권으로 구성되어 있습니다.
이 시리즈는 Grammar Mentor Joy 시리즈의 첫 단계로 처음 문법을 시작하는 학생들을 대상으로 문법에 흥미를 가질 수 있도록 구성되어 있습니다. 각 Level이 각각 8개의 Chapter 총 8주의 학습 시간으로 구성되어 있는데, 특히 Chapter가 끝나면 Final Check 문제와 Exercise를 두어 반복 복습을 할 수 있도록 하였습니다. 부가적으로 워크북과 단어테스트를 제공하고 있으며 한 레벨이 끝나면 자가 테스트를 할 수 있는 실전 모의고사 테스트도 각각 3회씩 제공되고 있습니다.

| Level | Month | Week | Chapter | Unit | Homework |
|---|---|---|---|---|---|
| 1 | 1st | 1 | 1 명사와 관사 | 01 명사 | 각 Chapter별 단어 퀴즈 제공<br>–<br>각 Chapter별 드릴 문제 제공 (워크북)<br>–<br>각 Chapter별 추가 문제 제공 (선생님용) |
| | | | | 02 명사의 복수형 | |
| | | 2 | 2 인칭대명사 I | 01 인칭대명사와 be동사 | |
| | | | | 02 주어+be동사+명사/장소 | |
| | | 3 | 3 형용사 | 01 형용사의 종류 | |
| | | | | 02 반대 의미의 형용사 | |
| | | 4 | 4 be동사의 부정문과 의문문 | 01 be동사의 부정문 | |
| | | | | 02 be동사의 의문문 | |
| | 2nd | 1 | 5 동사 | 01 일반동사 | 각 Chapter별 단어 퀴즈 제공<br>–<br>각 Chapter별 드릴 문제 제공 (워크북)<br>–<br>각 Chapter별 추가 문제 제공 (선생님용)<br>–<br>최종 3회의 실전모의고사 테스트지 제공 |
| | | | | 02 주어가 3인칭 단수일 때 동사의 변화 | |
| | | 2 | 6 일반동사의 부정문과 의문문 | 01 일반동사의 부정문 | |
| | | | | 02 일반동사의 의문문 | |
| | | 3 | 7 인칭대명사 II | 01 my / your / me / you | |
| | | | | 02 He / She / They / It의 쓰임 | |
| | | 4 | 8 can / be going to | 01 can의 쓰임 | |
| | | | | 02 be going to의 쓰임 | |

# 특징

1 학습자 눈높이에 맞춘 챕터 구성
2 단계별 학습을 통한 맞춤식 문법 학습
3 내신대비를 위한 서술형 문제 풀이 학습
4 단순 암기식 공부가 아닌 사고력이 필요한 문제 풀이 학습
5 반복적인 학습을 통한 문제 풀이 능력 향상
6 기초 어휘와 문장을 통한 체계적인 학습
7 반복적인 문제 풀이를 통한 자연스런 학습
8 초등 기초 문법을 완벽 마스터

| Level | Month | Week | Chapter | Unit | Homework |
|---|---|---|---|---|---|
| 2 | 3rd | 1 | 1 명사의 복수형과 셀 수 없는 명사 | 01 단수명사와 복수명사 | 각 Chapter별 단어 퀴즈 제공 – 각 Chapter별 드릴 문제 제공 (워크북) – 각 Chapter별 추가 문제 제공 (선생님용) |
| | | | | 02 셀 수 없는 명사 | |
| | | 2 | 2 정관사 the와 this, that | 01 정관사 the | |
| | | | | 02 this와 that | |
| | | 3 | 3 There is / There are | 01 There is / There are | |
| | | | | 02 There is / There are 부정문과 의문문 | |
| | | 4 | 4 현재진행형 | 01 현재진행형의 의미와 형태 | |
| | | | | 02 현재진행형의 부정문과 의문문 | |
| | 4th | 1 | 5 형용사와 부사 | 01 형용사 | 각 Chapter별 단어 퀴즈 제공 – 각 Chapter별 드릴 문제 제공 (워크북) – 각 Chapter별 추가 문제 제공 (선생님용) – 최종 3회의 실전모의고사 테스트지 제공 |
| | | | | 02 부사 | |
| | | 2 | 6 동사의 과거형 I | 01 be동사의 과거형 | |
| | | | | 02 일반동사 과거형 - 규칙 변화 | |
| | | 3 | 7 동사의 과거형 II | 01 일반동사 과거형 - 불규칙 변화 | |
| | | | | 02 일반동사 과거형 부정문과 의문문 | |
| | | 4 | 8 전치사 | 01 시간과 장소의 전치사 | |
| | | | | 02 위치의 전치사 | |

## Unit 설명 & Warm up

각 Chapter를 2개의 Unit으로 나누어 체계적으로 설명하고 있으며, Warm up에서는 본격적인 학습에 앞서 기본적인 내용을 한 번 더 확인할 수 있도록 했습니다.

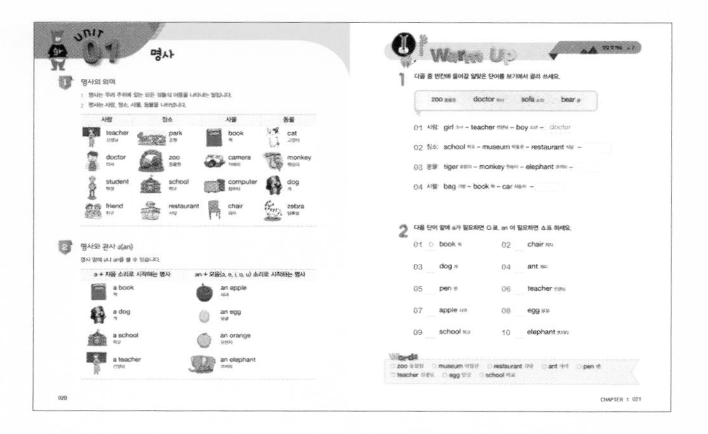

## Check up

각 Unit에서 다루고 있는 문법의 기본적인 내용들을 확인할 수 있도록 했습니다.

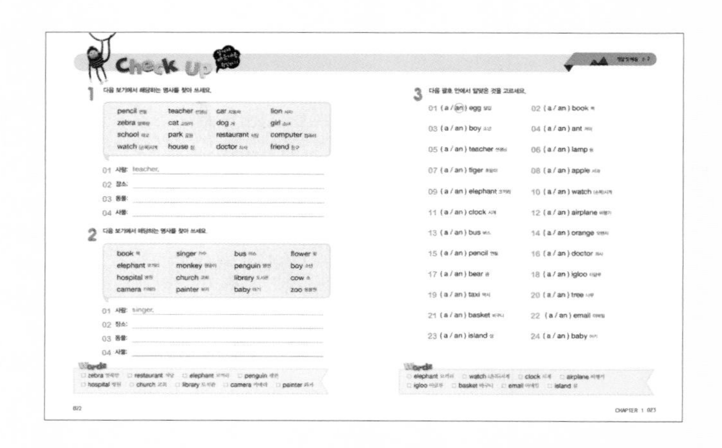

## Step up

각 Unit에서 배운 내용을 활용해서 다양한 유형의 문제 풀이를 할 수 있도록 했습니다.

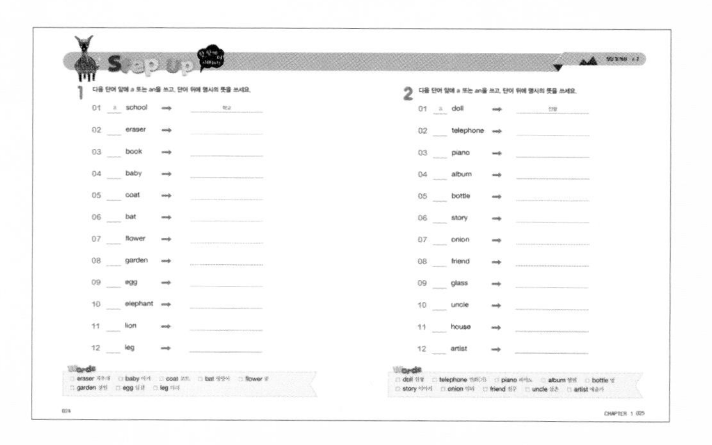

## Final Check

각 Chapter의 내용을 최종 점검하는 단계로 두 Unit의 내용들을 기초로 한 문제들로 구성되어 있습니다. 특히, Writing 실력을 향상할 수 있는 문제들을 추가하였습니다.

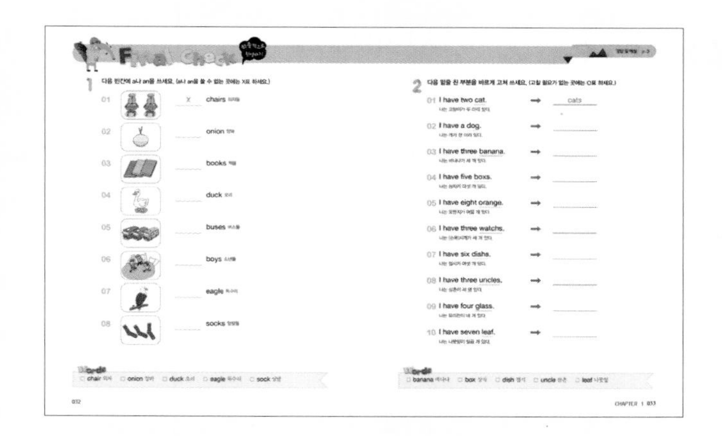

## Exercise

각 Chapter가 끝나면 시험에서 볼 수 있는 관련 문제 유형들을 다양하게 제시했습니다. 또한 앞서 배운 내용을 다시 한 번 복습할 수 있도록 구성했습니다.

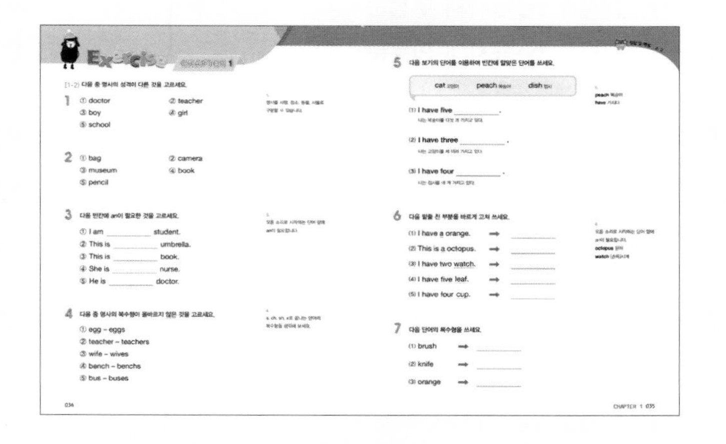

## 실전모의고사

총 3회로 구성되어 있으며 책에서 배운 모든 내용을 5지선다형 문제와 서술형 문제로 구성하여 학습자들이 최종적으로 학습한 내용을 점검할 수 있도록 했습니다.

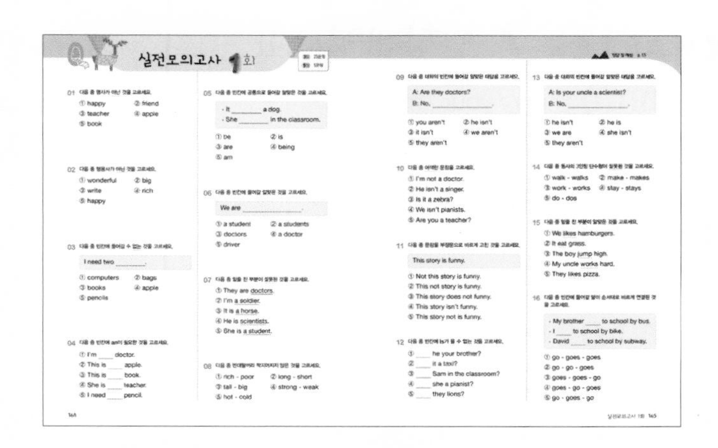

# Contents

Alphabet &
Consonants-Vowels

# Alphabet

## 알파벳은 무엇인가요?

우리말은 ㄱ, ㄴ, ㄷ, ㄹ, ㅁ, ㅂ, …… ㅏ, ㅓ, ㅗ, ㅜ, ㅡ, ㅣ가 모여 하나의 의미 단위 즉, 한 단어, 구, 문장을 만듭니다. 우리말의 한글 자음, 모음에 해당하는 것이 영어의 알파벳입니다. 알파벳이 모여 하나의 의미를 가진 단어, 구, 문장을 만듭니다.

| c, a, t → | cat → | a little cat → | I have a little cat. |
|---|---|---|---|
| 알파벳 | 단어 | 구 | 문장 |

→ 구 : 두 개 이상의 단어가 모여 문장의 일부분이 되는 단위입니다.

알파벳은 26개이고, 각각의 알파벳에는 대문자와 소문자가 있습니다.

1. 다음 빈칸에 알맞은 알파벳 대문자를 쓰세요.

2. 다음 빈칸에 알맞은 알파벳 소문자를 쓰세요.

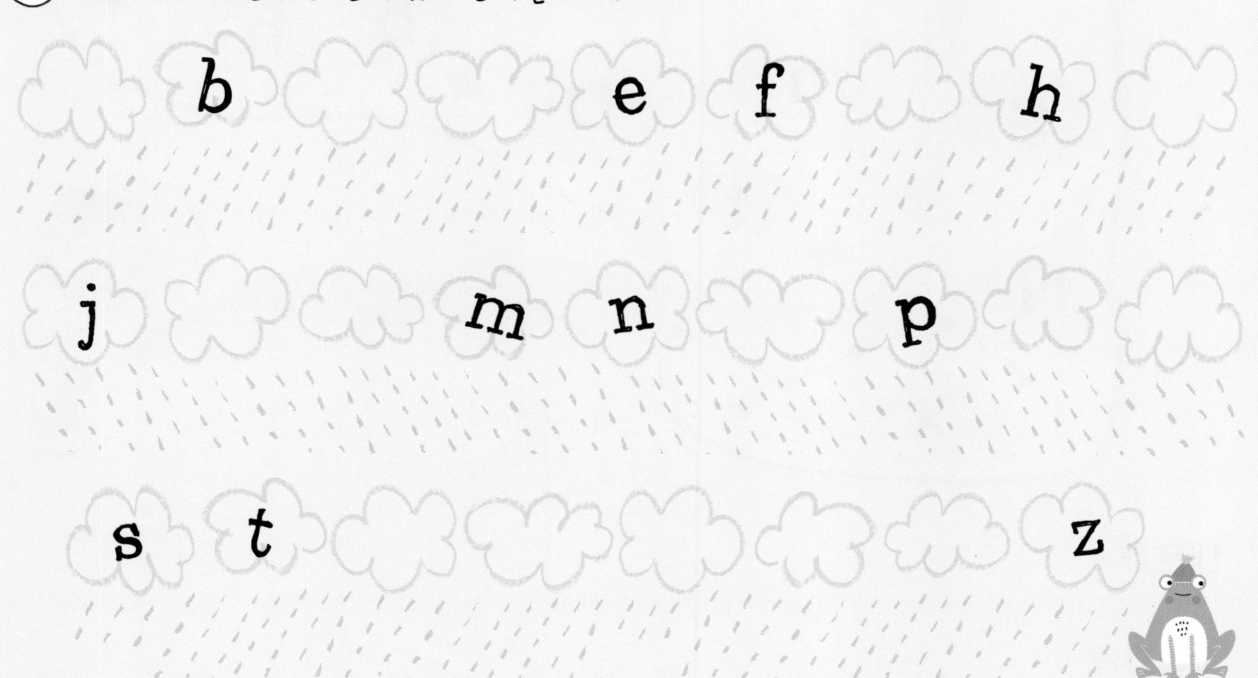

③ 다음 주어진 알파벳에서 대문자는 ◯, 소문자는 □ 표시하고, 아래 써 보세요.

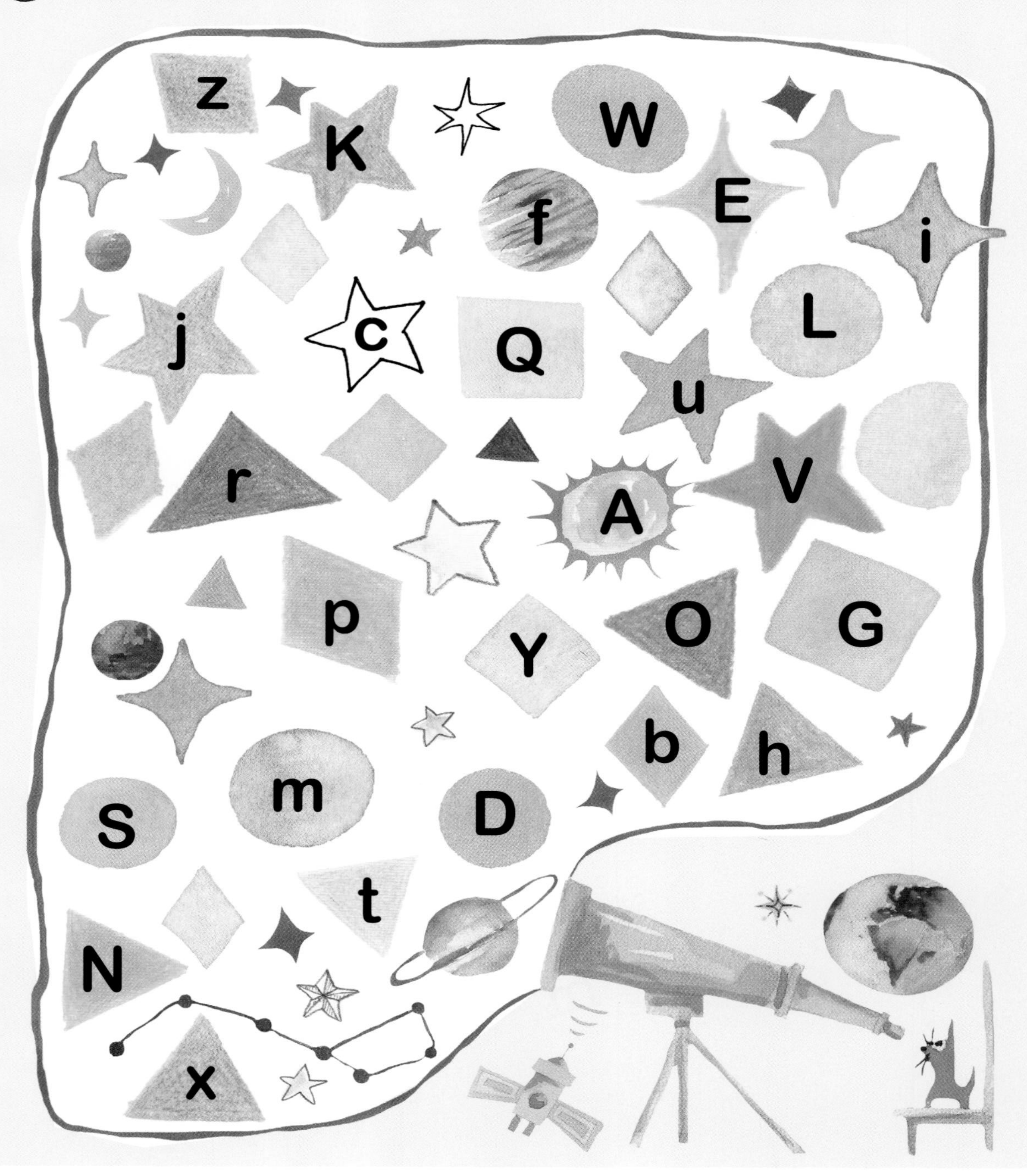


대문자

소문자

## ④ 다음 단어를 소문자로 바꿔 쓰세요.

01 BEAR 곰 ____________

02 BABY 아기 ____________

03 COOK 요리사 ____________

04 HOUSE 집 ____________

05 ALBUM 앨범 ____________

06 ZOO 동물원 ____________

07 TURTLE 거북 ____________

08 BUS 버스 ____________

09 FLOWER 꽃 ____________

10 RICH 부유한 ____________

11 SINGER 가수 ____________

12 BOTTLE 병 ____________

## ⑤ 다음 단어를 대문자로 바꿔 쓰세요.

01 sock 양말 ____________

02 tiger 호랑이 ____________

03 nice 멋진 ____________

04 ribbon 리본 ____________

05 green 녹색 ____________

06 egg 달걀 ____________

07 ant 개미 ____________

08 hungry 배고픈 ____________

09 leg 다리 ____________

10 nurse 간호사 ____________

11 carrot 당근 ____________

12 box 상자 ____________

자음과 모음

## 자음과 모음은 무엇인가요?

우리말 '컵'이라는 의미를 가진 소리는 어떻게 이루어져 있나요? 컵은 자음 'ㅋ'과 모음 'ㅓ', 그리고 자음 'ㅂ'이 결합하여 내는 소리입니다. 우리말이 자음(ㄱ, ㄴ, ㄷ …)과 모음(ㅏ, ㅓ, ㅗ …)이 결합하여 의미를 가진 소리를 만드는 것처럼 영어도 자음과 모음이 결합하여 의미를 가진 소리를 만듭니다.

한글 : 컵 = ㅋ(자음) + ㅓ(모음) + ㅂ(자음)

영어 : cup = c(자음) + u(모음) + p(자음)

영어는 자음 21개와 모음 5개가 있습니다.

★ 영어의 자음 : b, c, d, f, g, h, j, k, l, m, n, p, q, r, s, t, v, w, x, y, z (모음을 뺀 나머지)

★ 영어의 모음 : a, e, i, o, u

영어에서 cup이라는 단어는 알파벳 자음 'c', 모음 'u', 자음 'p'가 결합하여 만들어집니다. 이처럼 자음과 모음의 조합으로 수많은 단어들이 만들어지고, 이 단어들이 모여 언어를 구성합니다. 따라서, 문장을 구성하는 규칙인 '문법'을 공부하기 전에 자음과 모음을 정확히 익히는 것이 중요합니다.

1 다음 알파벳에서 모음을 찾아 동그라미 하세요.

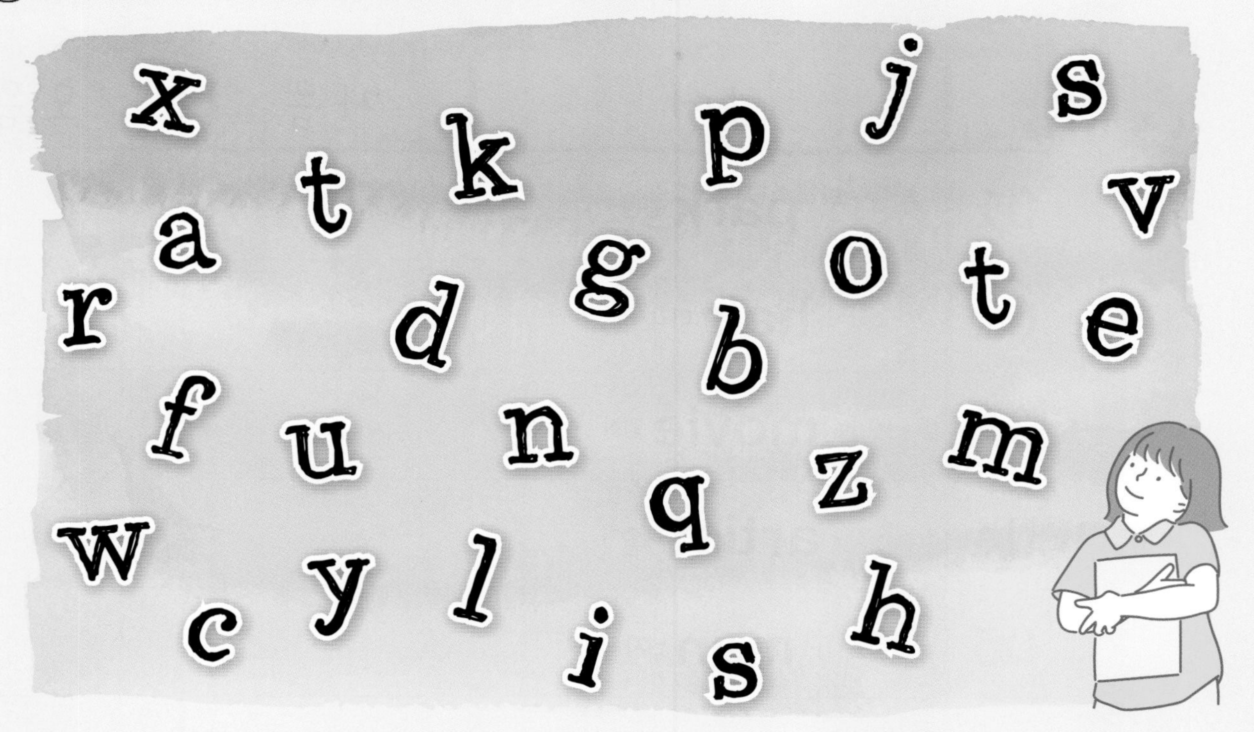


2 다음 단어에서 모음을 찾아 동그라미 하세요.

| | | | | | |
|---|---|---|---|---|---|
| 01 | uncle | 삼촌 | 02 | angry | 화난 |
| 03 | strong | 강인한 | 04 | island | 섬 |
| 05 | knife | 칼 | 06 | bird | 새 |
| 07 | driver | 운전자 | 08 | zebra | 얼룩말 |
| 09 | onion | 양파 | 10 | brush | 붓 |
| 11 | round | 둥근 | 12 | cousin | 사촌 |

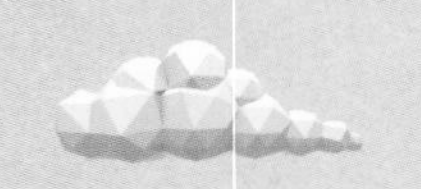

③ 다음 단어에서 모음과 자음을 나눠 쓰세요.

| | 단어 | 자음 | 모음 |
|---|---|---|---|
| 01 | park 공원 | | |
| 02 | hair 머리카락 | | |
| 03 | movie 영화 | | |
| 04 | artist 예술가 | | |
| 05 | man 남자 | | |
| 06 | ten 10 | | |
| 07 | room 방 | | |
| 08 | animal 동물 | | |
| 09 | pencil 연필 | | |
| 10 | watch 시계 | | |
| 11 | leaf 나뭇잎 | | |
| 12 | snake 뱀 | | |

① 영어의 알파벳을 소문자로 쓰고, 모음에 동그라미 하세요.

② 다음 〈보기〉와 같이 단어를 분리하고, 자음인지 모음인지 구별하여 쓰세요.

**king** 왕 = k + i + n + g
(k 자음, i 모음, n 자음, g 자음)

01 **friend** 친구 = ___ + ___ + ___ + ___ + ___ + ___

02 **actor** 배우 = ___ + ___ + ___ + ___ + ___

03 **long** 긴 = ___ + ___ + ___ + ___

04 **doll** 인형 = ___ + ___ + ___ + ___

05 **tomato** 토마토 = ___ + ___ + ___ + ___ + ___ + ___

## Alphabet

### Check up p.011

① C, E, F, H, J, M, N, P, Q, T, U, V, X, Z

② a, c, d, g, i, k, l, o, q, r, u, v, w, x, y

③

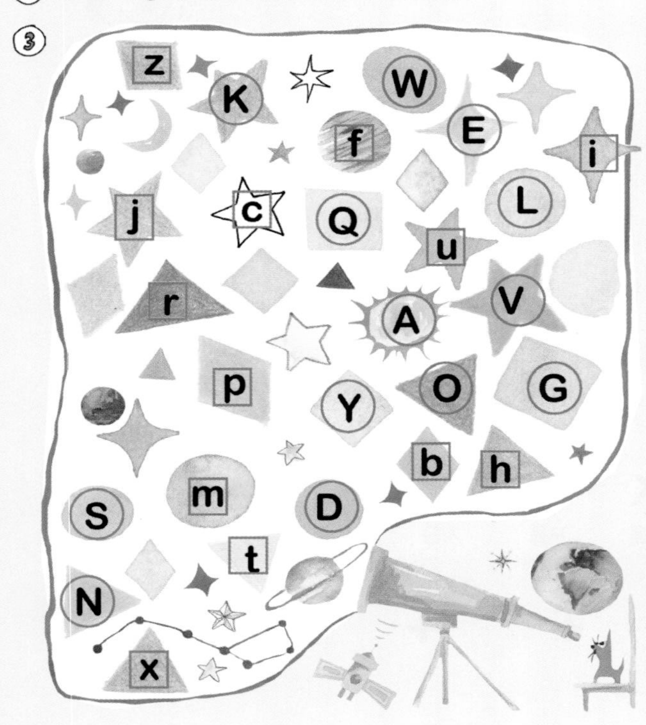


**대문자** A, D, E, G, K, L, N, O, Q, S, V, W, Y

**소문자** b, c, f, h, i, j, m, p, r, t, u, x, z

④ 01 bear 02 baby 03 cook
04 house 05 album 06 zoo
07 turtle 08 bus 09 flower
10 rich 11 singer 12 bottle

⑤ 01 SOCK 02 TIGER 03 NICE
04 RIBBON 05 GREEN 06 EGG
07 ANT 08 HUNGRY 09 LEG
10 NURSE 11 CARROT 12 BOX

## Consonants and Vowels

### Check up p.015

①

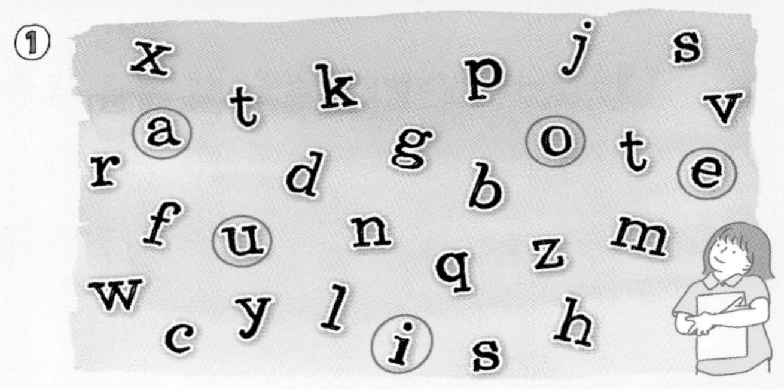


② 01 u, e 02 a 03 o 04 i, a 05 i, e 06 i 07 i, e
08 e, a 09 o, i, o 10 u 11 o, u 12 o, u, i

③

| | 단어 | 자음 | 모음 |
|---|---|---|---|
| 01 | park 공원 | p, r, k | a |
| 02 | hair 머리카락 | h, r | a, i |
| 03 | movie 영화 | m, v | o, i, e |
| 04 | artist 예술가 | r, t, s, t | a, i |
| 05 | man 남자 | m, n | a |
| 06 | ten 10 | t, n | e |
| 07 | room 방 | r, m | o, o |
| 08 | animal 동물 | n, m, l | a, i, a |
| 09 | pencil 연필 | p. n ,c, l | e, i |
| 10 | watch 시계 | w, t, c, h | a |
| 11 | leaf 나뭇잎 | l, f | e, a |
| 12 | snake 뱀 | s, n, k | a, e |

### Wrap up p.017

① ⓐ, b, c, d, ⓔ, f, g, h, ⓘ, j, k, l, m, n,
ⓞ, p, q, r, s, t, ⓤ, v, w, x, y, z

② 01 friend = f + r + i + e + n + d
자음 자음 모음 모음 자음 자음

02 actor = a + c + t + o + r
모음 자음 자음 모음 자음

03 long = l + o + n + g
자음 모음 자음 자음

04 doll = d + o + l + l
자음 모음 자음 자음

05 tomato = t + o + m + a + t + o
자음 모음 자음 모음 자음 모음

# CHAPTER 1
# 명사와 관사

# 명사

## 명사의 의미

1 명사는 우리 주위에 있는 모든 것들의 이름을 나타내는 말입니다.

2 명사는 사람, 장소, 사물, 동물 등을 나타냅니다.

| 사람 | 장소 | 사물 | 동물 |
|---|---|---|---|
| teacher 선생님 | park 공원 | book 책 | cat 고양이 |
| doctor 의사 | zoo 동물원 | camera 카메라 | monkey 원숭이 |
| student 학생 | school 학교 | computer 컴퓨터 | dog 개 |
| friend 친구 | restaurant 식당 | chair 의자 | zebra 얼룩말 |

## 명사와 관사 a(an)

명사 앞에 a나 an을 쓸 수 있습니다.

| a + 자음 소리로 시작하는 명사 | an + 모음(a, e, i, o, u) 소리로 시작하는 명사 |
|---|---|
| a book 책 | an apple 사과 |
| a dog 개 | an egg 달걀 |
| a school 학교 | an orange 오렌지 |
| a teacher 선생님 | an elephant 코끼리 |

# Warm Up

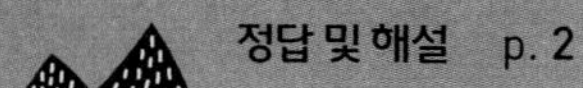
정답 및 해설 p. 2

## 1 다음 중 빈칸에 들어갈 알맞은 단어를 보기에서 골라 쓰세요.

zoo 동물원 doctor 의사 sofa 소파 bear 곰

01 사람: girl 소녀 – teacher 선생님 – boy 소년 – doctor

02 장소: school 학교 – museum 박물관 – restaurant 식당 – ______

03 동물: tiger 호랑이 – monkey 원숭이 – elephant 코끼리 – ______

04 사물: bag 가방 – book 책 – car 자동차 – ______

## 2 다음 단어 앞에 a가 필요하면 ○표, an 이 필요하면 △표 하세요.

01 ○ book 책

02 ___ chair 의자

03 ___ dog 개

04 ___ ant 개미

05 ___ pen 펜

06 ___ teacher 선생님

07 ___ apple 사과

08 ___ egg 달걀

09 ___ school 학교

10 ___ elephant 코끼리

### Words

□ zoo 동물원 □ museum 박물관 □ restaurant 식당 □ ant 개미 □ pen 펜
□ teacher 선생님 □ egg 달걀 □ school 학교

## 1 다음 보기에서 해당하는 명사를 찾아 쓰세요.

| | | | |
|---|---|---|---|
| pencil 연필 | teacher 선생님 | car 자동차 | lion 사자 |
| zebra 얼룩말 | cat 고양이 | dog 개 | girl 소녀 |
| school 학교 | park 공원 | restaurant 식당 | computer 컴퓨터 |
| watch (손목)시계 | house 집 | doctor 의사 | friend 친구 |

01 사람: teacher, ____________________

02 장소: ____________________

03 동물: ____________________

04 사물: ____________________

## 2 다음 보기에서 해당하는 명사를 찾아 쓰세요.

| | | | |
|---|---|---|---|
| book 책 | singer 가수 | bus 버스 | flower 꽃 |
| elephant 코끼리 | monkey 원숭이 | penguin 펭귄 | boy 소년 |
| hospital 병원 | church 교회 | library 도서관 | cow 소 |
| camera 카메라 | painter 화가 | baby 아기 | zoo 동물원 |

01 사람: singer, ____________________

02 장소: ____________________

03 동물: ____________________

04 사물: ____________________

**Words**

☐ zebra 얼룩말 ☐ restaurant 식당 ☐ elephant 코끼리 ☐ penguin 펭귄
☐ hospital 병원 ☐ church 교회 ☐ library 도서관 ☐ camera 카메라 ☐ painter 화가

## 3 다음 괄호 안에서 알맞은 것을 고르세요.

01 ( a / an ) egg 달걀
02 ( a / an ) book 책
03 ( a / an ) boy 소년
04 ( a / an ) ant 개미
05 ( a / an ) teacher 선생님
06 ( a / an ) lamp 등
07 ( a / an ) tiger 호랑이
08 ( a / an ) apple 사과
09 ( a / an ) elephant 코끼리
10 ( a / an ) watch (손목)시계
11 ( a / an ) clock 시계
12 ( a / an ) airplane 비행기
13 ( a / an ) bus 버스
14 ( a / an ) orange 오렌지
15 ( a / an ) pencil 연필
16 ( a / an ) doctor 의사
17 ( a / an ) bear 곰
18 ( a / an ) igloo 이글루
19 ( a / an ) taxi 택시
20 ( a / an ) tree 나무
21 ( a / an ) basket 바구니
22 ( a / an ) email 이메일
23 ( a / an ) island 섬
24 ( a / an ) baby 아기

**Words**

□ elephant 코끼리 □ watch (손목)시계 □ clock 시계 □ airplane 비행기
□ igloo 이글루 □ basket 바구니 □ email 이메일 □ island 섬

# Step Up

한 단계 더 이해하기

**1** 다음 단어 앞에 a 또는 an을 쓰고, 단어 뒤에 명사의 뜻을 쓰세요.

01 __a__ school → 학교

02 ____ eraser → ________

03 ____ book → ________

04 ____ baby → ________

05 ____ coat → ________

06 ____ bat → ________

07 ____ flower → ________

08 ____ garden → ________

09 ____ egg → ________

10 ____ elephant → ________

11 ____ lion → ________

12 ____ leg → ________

**Words**

☐ eraser 지우개 ☐ baby 아기 ☐ coat 코트 ☐ bat 방망이 ☐ flower 꽃
☐ garden 정원 ☐ egg 달걀 ☐ leg 다리

정답 및 해설 p. 2

## 2 다음 단어 앞에 a 또는 an을 쓰고, 단어 뒤에 명사의 뜻을 쓰세요.

01 __a__ doll → 인형

02 ____ telephone → ____________

03 ____ piano → ____________

04 ____ album → ____________

05 ____ bottle → ____________

06 ____ story → ____________

07 ____ onion → ____________

08 ____ friend → ____________

09 ____ glass → ____________

10 ____ uncle → ____________

11 ____ house → ____________

12 ____ artist → ____________

**Words**

□ doll 인형 □ telephone 전화(기) □ piano 피아노 □ album 앨범 □ bottle 병
□ story 이야기 □ onion 양파 □ friend 친구 □ uncle 삼촌 □ artist 예술가

# UNIT 02 명사의 복수형

## 1 명사의 복수형 만들기

1 명사 뒤에 s 또는 es를 붙여 명사의 복수형을 만듭니다.

2 복수라는 것은 사람, 물건, 동물 등이 2명 또는 2개 이상을 의미합니다.

| 명사 + s | 명사 + es |
|---|---|
| a cat – cats<br>고양이 고양이들 | a watch – watches<br>(손목)시계 (손목)시계들 |
| a book – books<br>책 책들 | a bus – buses<br>버스 버스들 |

**TIPS** s 또는 es가 붙은 복수명사 앞에는 a나 an을 쓸 수 없습니다.
- **a watches (x)** · **an ants (x)**

## 2 명사의 복수형 만드는 법

1 대부분의 명사에 s를 붙입니다.

2 s, ch, sh, x로 끝나는 명사에는 es를 붙입니다.

3 f나 fe로 끝나면 f나 fe를 v로 바꾸고 es를 붙입니다.

| | | | |
|---|---|---|---|
| **대부분의 명사** | dog – dogs<br>개 개들 | cat – cats<br>고양이 고양이들 | tiger – tigers<br>호랑이 호랑이들 |
| | girl – girls<br>소녀 소녀들 | school – schools<br>학교 학교들 | picture – pictures<br>그림 그림들 |
| **s, ch, sh, x로 끝나는 명사** | bus – buses<br>버스 버스들 | bench – benches<br>벤치 벤치들 | church – churches<br>교회 교회들 |
| | box – boxes<br>상자 상자들 | dish – dishes<br>접시 접시들 | brush – brushes<br>붓 붓들 |
| **f나 fe로 끝나는 명사** | wolf – wolves<br>늑대 늑대들 | leaf – leaves<br>나뭇잎 나뭇잎들 | thief – thieves<br>도둑 도둑들 |

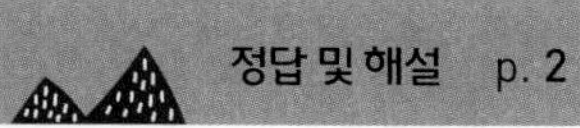
정답 및 해설 p. 2

## 1 다음 빈칸에 a나 an을 쓰세요. a나 an을 쓸 수 없는 복수형에는 X표 하세요.

01 ___X___ pencils 연필들

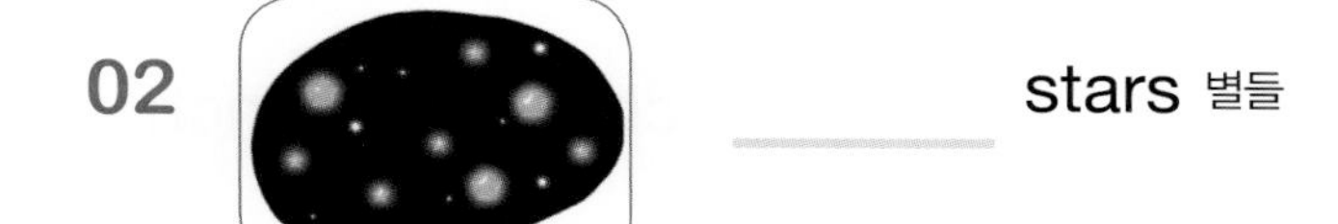

02 ______ stars 별들

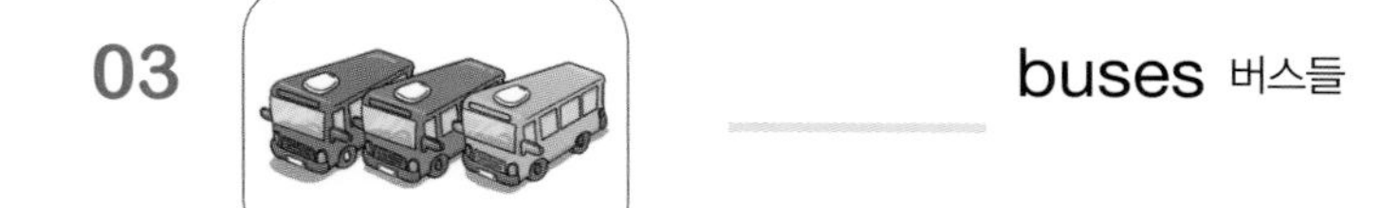

03 ______ buses 버스들

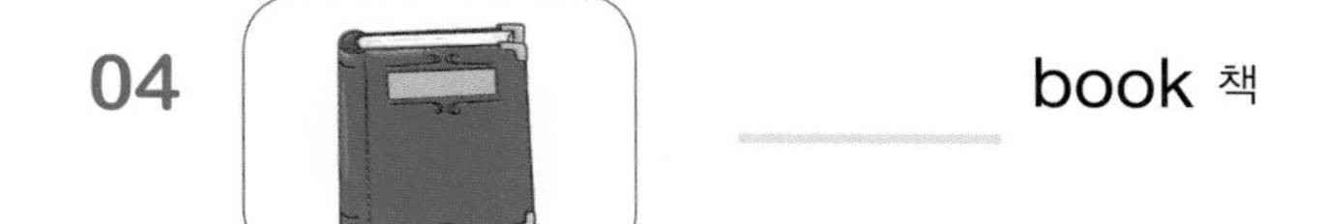

04 ______ book 책

05 ______ umbrellas 우산들

06 ______ cow 소

07 ______ girls 소녀들

08 ______ orange 오렌지

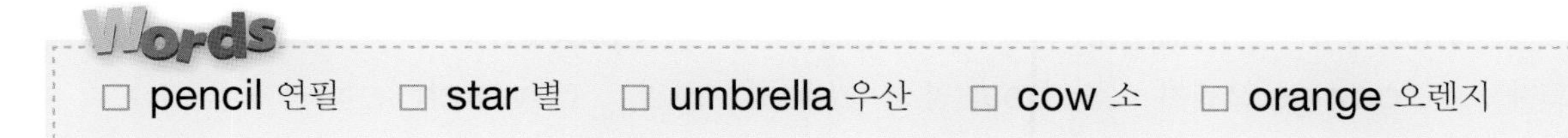

**Words**

□ pencil 연필 □ star 별 □ umbrella 우산 □ cow 소 □ orange 오렌지

## 1 다음 빈칸에 알맞은 말을 넣고 복수형을 만들어 보세요.

| | | | | |
|---|---|---|---|---|
| ring 반지 | wife 아내 | box 상자 | church 교회 | dog 개 |
| cat 고양이 | thief 도둑 | tiger 호랑이 | bird 새 | bus 버스 |
| boy 소년 | wolf 늑대 | dish 접시 | picture 그림 | cap 야구모자 |
| orange 오렌지 | bear 곰 | leaf 나뭇잎 | watch (손목)시계 | bench 벤치 |

**01** 대부분의 명사 ➡ 복수형: 명사+s

ring ➡ rings　　＿＿＿＿ ➡ ＿＿＿＿

＿＿＿＿ ➡ ＿＿＿＿　　＿＿＿＿ ➡ ＿＿＿＿

＿＿＿＿ ➡ ＿＿＿＿　　＿＿＿＿ ➡ ＿＿＿＿

＿＿＿＿ ➡ ＿＿＿＿　　＿＿＿＿ ➡ ＿＿＿＿

＿＿＿＿ ➡ ＿＿＿＿　　＿＿＿＿ ➡ ＿＿＿＿

**02** s, ch, sh, x로 끝나는 명사 ➡ 복수형: 명사+es

box ➡ boxes　　＿＿＿＿ ➡ ＿＿＿＿

＿＿＿＿ ➡ ＿＿＿＿　　＿＿＿＿ ➡ ＿＿＿＿

＿＿＿＿ ➡ ＿＿＿＿　　＿＿＿＿ ➡ ＿＿＿＿

**03** f나 fe로 끝나는 명사 ➡ 복수형: f나 fe를 v로 바꾸고 es

wife ➡ wives　　＿＿＿＿ ➡ ＿＿＿＿

＿＿＿＿ ➡ ＿＿＿＿　　＿＿＿＿ ➡ ＿＿＿＿

**Words**

☐ ring 반지　☐ wife 아내　☐ church 교회　☐ thief 도둑　☐ picture 그림
☐ cap 야구모자　☐ orange 오렌지　☐ bear 곰　☐ leaf 나뭇잎　☐ watch (손목)시계

## 2 다음 괄호 안에서 명사의 올바른 복수형을 고르세요.

01 dog 개 ➡ ( dogs / doges )

02 cat 고양이 ➡ ( cats / cates )

03 bus 버스 ➡ ( buss / buses )

04 dish 접시 ➡ ( dishs / dishes )

05 tiger 호랑이 ➡ ( tigers / tigeres )

06 box 상자 ➡ ( boxes / boxies )

07 wolf 늑대 ➡ ( wolfes / wolves )

08 student 학생 ➡ ( students / studentes )

09 leaf 나뭇잎 ➡ ( leafes / leaves )

10 school 학교 ➡ ( schools / schooles )

11 girl 소녀 ➡ ( girls / girles )

12 bench 벤치 ➡ ( benchs / benches )

☐ bus 버스 ☐ dish 접시 ☐ tiger 호랑이 ☐ wolf 늑대 ☐ bench 벤치

## 1 다음 중 옳은 표현에 O표 하세요.

| | | | | |
|---|---|---|---|---|
| 01 | three rat | ___ | three rats | O |
| 02 | two benchs | ___ | two benches | ___ |
| 03 | one egg | ___ | one eggs | ___ |
| 04 | nine boxs | ___ | nine boxes | ___ |
| 05 | four watchs | ___ | four watches | ___ |
| 06 | two tiger | ___ | two tigers | ___ |
| 07 | three boys | ___ | three boyes | ___ |
| 08 | eight brushs | ___ | eight brushes | ___ |

**Words**

□ rat 쥐 □ egg 달걀 □ watch (손목)시계 □ tiger 호랑이 □ brush 붓

## 2 다음 보기의 단어를 이용하여 빈칸에 알맞은 영어를 쓰세요.

| | | | | | | |
|---|---|---|---|---|---|---|
| 숫자 | two 둘 | three 셋 | four 넷 | five 다섯 | six 여섯 | ten 열 |
| 명사 | apple 사과 | dish 접시 | glass 유리잔 | | | |
| | leaf 나뭇잎 | box 상자 | knife 칼 | | | |

01 three apples

02 ________ ________

03 ________ ________

04 ________ ________

05 ________ ________

06 ________ ________

**Words**

☐ four 넷 ☐ ten 열 ☐ dish 접시 ☐ glass 유리잔 ☐ leaf 나뭇잎 ☐ knife 칼

## 1 다음 빈칸에 a나 an을 쓰세요. (a나 an을 쓸 수 없는 곳에는 X표 하세요.)

01 ___X___ chairs 의자들

02 ______ onion 양파

03 ______ books 책들

04 ______ duck 오리

05 ______ buses 버스들

06 ______ boys 소년들

07 ______ eagle 독수리

08 ______ socks 양말들

## 2 다음 밑줄 친 부분을 바르게 고쳐 쓰세요. (고칠 필요가 없는 곳에는 O표 하세요.)

01 I have two cat. → cats
나는 고양이가 두 마리 있다.

02 I have a dog. → ________
나는 개가 한 마리 있다.

03 I have three banana. → ________
나는 바나나가 세 개 있다.

04 I have five boxs. → ________
나는 상자가 다섯 개 있다.

05 I have eight orange. → ________
나는 오렌지가 여덟 개 있다.

06 I have three watchs. → ________
나는 (손목)시계가 세 개 있다.

07 I have six dishs. → ________
나는 접시가 여섯 개 있다.

08 I have three uncles. → ________
나는 삼촌이 세 명 있다.

09 I have four glass. → ________
나는 유리잔이 네 개 있다.

10 I have seven leaf. → ________
나는 나뭇잎이 일곱 개 있다.

**Words**
□ banana 바나나 □ box 상자 □ dish 접시 □ uncle 삼촌 □ leaf 나뭇잎

[1-2] 다음 중 명사의 성격이 다른 것을 고르세요.

**1**
① doctor ② teacher
③ boy ④ girl
⑤ school

**2**
① bag ② camera
③ museum ④ book
⑤ pencil

**3** 다음 빈칸에 an이 필요한 것을 고르세요.

① I am ____________ student.
② This is ____________ umbrella.
③ This is ____________ book.
④ She is ____________ nurse.
⑤ He is ____________ doctor.

**4** 다음 중 명사의 복수형이 올바르지 않은 것을 고르세요.

① egg – eggs
② teacher – teachers
③ wife – wives
④ bench – benchs
⑤ bus – buses

1.
명사를 사람, 장소, 동물, 사물로 구분할 수 있습니다.

3.
모음 소리로 시작하는 단어 앞에 an이 필요합니다.

4.
s, ch, sh, x로 끝나는 단어의 복수형을 생각해 보세요.

## 5 다음 보기의 단어를 이용하여 빈칸에 알맞은 단어를 쓰세요.

cat 고양이  peach 복숭아  dish 접시

(1) **I have five ______________.**
나는 복숭아를 다섯 개 가지고 있다.

(2) **I have three ______________.**
나는 고양이를 세 마리 가지고 있다.

(3) **I have four ______________.**
나는 접시를 네 개 가지고 있다.

5.
**peach** 복숭아
**have** 가지다

## 6 다음 밑줄 친 부분을 바르게 고쳐 쓰세요.

(1) I have a orange. ➡ ______________
(2) This is a octopus. ➡ ______________
(3) I have two watch. ➡ ______________
(4) I have five leaf. ➡ ______________
(5) I have four cup. ➡ ______________

6.
모음 소리로 시작하는 단어 앞에 an이 필요합니다.
**octopus** 문어
**watch** (손목)시계

## 7 다음 단어의 복수형을 쓰세요.

(1) brush ➡ ______________
(2) knife ➡ ______________
(3) orange ➡ ______________

다음 단어의 뜻을 쓰고, 단어를 더 써보세요.

| | | | | | | | |
|---|---|---|---|---|---|---|---|
| 01 | album | 앨범 | album | 02 | ant | | |
| 03 | artist | | | 04 | bench | | |
| 05 | bottle | | | 06 | brush | | |
| 07 | church | | | 08 | clock | | |
| 09 | doll | | | 10 | egg | | |
| 11 | flower | | | 12 | igloo | | |
| 13 | island | | | 14 | knife | | |
| 15 | leaf | | | 16 | leg | | |
| 17 | museum | | | 18 | onion | | |
| 19 | orange | | | 20 | park | | |
| 21 | pencil | | | 22 | sock | | |
| 23 | teacher | | | 24 | telephone | | |
| 25 | tiger | | | 26 | umbrella | | |
| 27 | uncle | | | 28 | watch | | |
| 29 | zebra | | | 30 | zoo | | |

# CHAPTER 2
# 인칭대명사 I

UNIT 01 인칭대명사와 be동사
UNIT 02 주어+be동사+명사/장소

# 인칭대명사와 be동사

## 인칭대명사

1 대명사는 앞서 말한 사람 · 사물 · 동물 등을 대신하는 말로, 말하는 사람과 듣는 사람이 서로 알고 있는 명사에 대해 말할 때 사용합니다.

2 인칭대명사란 사람 또는 사물을 나타내는 대명사를 말합니다.

3 인칭대명사 중 주어 자리에 오는 인칭대명사를 주격이라고 합니다.

| **단수 인칭대명사** (한 사람 또는 한 개)<br>I / You / He / She / It (주어 역할) | | **복수 인칭대명사** (두 명 이상 또는 두 개 이상)<br>We / You / They (주어 역할) | |
|---|---|---|---|
| I 나는 | You 너는 | We 우리는 | You 너희들은 |
| He 그는(남성)<br>She 그녀는(여성) | It 그것은 | They 그들은(사람) | They 그것들은(사물) |

**TIPS** They는 두 사람 이상을 나타내거나 두 개 이상의 사물이나 동물을 나타낼 때 사용합니다.
- **They are students.** 그들은 학생들이다. • **They are books.** 그것들은 책들이다.

주어 역할을 하는 인칭대명사(주격)가 문장 처음에 나올 때에는 반드시 대문자로 써야 합니다.
- **they are books. (X)** • **They are books. (O)** 그것들은 책들이다.

## be동사의 쓰임

인칭대명사 다음에 오는 am, is, are를 be동사라고 합니다.

| | | |
|---|---|---|
| **am** | 주어가 I(나는)일 때만 사용합니다. | I am ~. |
| **are** | 주어가 You, We, They 그리고 복수형 명사(boys, teachers, students, friends 등)일 때 사용합니다. | You/We/They are ~. |
| **is** | 주어가 He, She, It일 때 사용합니다. | He/She/It is ~. |

**TIPS** is는 주어가 단수명사(a dog, a cat, Tom 등)일 때도 사용합니다. ⓔ A dog is ~ .

## be동사 축약

be동사는 다음과 같이 줄여서 사용할 수 있습니다. 보통 원어민들은 말할 때 이처럼 줄여서 사용합니다.

| | | |
|---|---|---|
| I am = **I'm** | You are = **You're** | He/She is = **He's / She's** |
| They are = **They're** | It is = **It's** | We are = **We're** |

# Warm Up

정답 및 해설 p. 3

**1** 다음 인칭대명사의 뜻과 관련된 것에 동그라미 하세요.

| | | | |
|---|---|---|---|
| 01 | I → | (나는) / 너는 / 우리는 | (단수) / 복수 |
| 02 | She → | 나는 / 그녀는 / 그는 | 단수 / 복수 |
| 03 | He → | 나는 / 그녀는 / 그는 | 단수 / 복수 |
| 04 | You → | 나는 / 그들은 / 너는 | 단수 / 복수 |
| 05 | We → | 우리는 / 그것은 / 너희들은 | 단수 / 복수 |
| 06 | It → | 나는 / 그것은 / 우리는 | 단수 / 복수 |
| 07 | You → | 나는 / 우리는 / 너희들은 | 단수 / 복수 |
| 08 | They → | 그는 / 그들은 / 우리는 | 단수 / 복수 |
| 09 | They → | 그는 / 그것은 / 그것들은 | 단수 / 복수 |

**Words**

☐ she 그녀 ☐ he 그 ☐ it 그것 ☐ they 그들, 그것들

## 1 다음 괄호 안에서 알맞은 것을 고르세요.

01 나는 요리사다. → I ( is / am / are ) a cook.

02 그것들은 양말들이다. → ( It / You / They ) are socks.

03 우리는 학생들이다. → We ( am / is / are ) students.

04 그것은 컴퓨터다. → It ( am / is / are ) a computer.

05 너희들은 가수들이다. → ( He / You / They ) are singers.

06 그는 배우다. → ( He / She / It ) is an actor.

07 그녀는 여왕이다. → She ( am / is / are ) a queen.

08 그는 무용수다. → He ( am / is / are ) a dancer.

09 그것은 달력이다. → ( He / She / It ) is a calendar.

10 그들은 내 친구들이다. → ( You / We / They ) are my friends.

11 그것들은 오렌지들이다. → ( It / You / They ) are oranges.

12 그것은 고양이다. → ( It / You / They ) is a cat.

**Words**

□ cook 요리사 □ computer 컴퓨터 □ singer 가수 □ actor 배우 □ queen 여왕
□ calendar 달력 □ friend 친구

## 2 다음 빈칸에 알맞은 be동사를 쓰세요.

**01** 고양이는 동물이다.

➡ A cat ___is___ an animal.

**02** 그것은 컴퓨터다.

➡ It ________ a computer.

**03** 기차는 매우 빠르다.

➡ A train ________ very fast.

**04** 사과들은 맛있다.

➡ Apples ________ delicious.

**05** 그들은 나의 학급 친구들이다.

➡ They ________ my classmates.

**06** 그녀는 내 엄마다.

➡ She ________ my mom.

**07** 코끼리는 큰 동물이다.

➡ An elephant ________ a big animal.

**08** 너는 좋은 선생님이다.

➡ You ________ a good teacher.

**09** 나는 컴퓨터 프로그래머다.

➡ I ________ a computer programmer.

**10** 그는 간호사다.

➡ He ________ a nurse.

**Words**

□ animal 동물 □ train 기차 □ delicious 맛있는 □ classmate 학급 친구
□ elephant 코끼리 □ computer programmer 컴퓨터 프로그래머 □ nurse 간호사

# Step Up

## 1 다음 빈칸에 알맞은 be동사나 인칭대명사를 쓰세요.

01 나는 왕이다. → I ___am___ a king.

02 그것들은 쿠키들이다. → They ________ cookies.

03 우리는 의사들이다. → We ________ doctors.

04 그것은 자전거다. → ________ is a bicycle.

05 너희들은 학생들이다. → You ________ students.

06 그들은 내 친구들이다. → They ________ my friends.

07 그는 소방관이다. → ________ is a firefighter.

08 그녀는 무용수다. → She ________ a dancer.

09 그것은 휴대전화다. → It ________ a cell phone.

10 너는 학생이다. → ________ are a student.

11 그것은 양파다. → It ________ an onion.

12 우리는 형제다. → ________ are brothers.

**Words**

□ king 왕 □ cookie 쿠키 □ bicycle 자전거 □ firefighter 소방관 □ dancer 무용수
□ cell phone 휴대전화(기) □ onion 양파 □ brother 형제

정답 및 해설 p. 3

## 2 다음 빈칸에 알맞은 be동사나 인칭대명사를 쓰세요.

01 그녀는 메리다. ➡ She is Mary.

02 톰은 학생이다. ➡ Tom ________ a student.

03 우리는 야구 선수들이다. ➡ We ________ baseball players.

04 그것은 책이다. ➡ ________ is a book.

05 그것들은 나뭇잎들이다. ➡ They ________ leaves.

06 그들은 내 사촌들이다. ➡ ________ are my cousins.

07 그는 택시 운전사다. ➡ ________ is a taxi driver.

08 그녀는 변호사다. ➡ She ________ a lawyer.

09 그것은 칼이다. ➡ It ________ a knife.

10 너희들은 매우 친절하다. ➡ ________ are very kind.

11 그들은 자매다. ➡ They ________ sisters.

12 그는 나의 선생님이다. ➡ ________ is my teacher.

**Words**

□ baseball player 야구 선수 □ cousin 사촌 □ taxi driver 택시 운전사 □ lawyer 변호사
□ knife 칼 □ sister 자매

# 인칭대명사+be동사+명사/장소

## 1 be동사의 의미

| be동사+명사 | ~이다 | He is a teacher. 그는 선생님이다. |
|---|---|---|
| be동사+장소 | ~(에) 있다 | She is in the room. 그녀는 방에 있다. |

## 2 be동사+명사

| 인칭대명사(단수)+be동사+단수명사 | 인칭대명사(복수)+be동사+복수명사 |
|---|---|
| I am a doctor. 나는 의사다. | We are doctors. 우리는 의사들이다. |
| You are a student. 너는 학생이다. | You are students. 너희들은 학생들이다. |
| She is a teacher. 그녀는 선생님이다. | They are teachers. 그들은 선생님들이다. |
| It is a cat. 그것은 고양이다. | They are cats. 그것들은 고양이들이다. |

TIPS **They are oranges.** 그것들은 오렌지들이다.
- 여기서 they는 사람이 아닌 사물을 표현합니다.
- they는 2개 이상을 나타내므로 orange도 복수형(oranges)으로 써야 합니다.

**She is teachers. (x)**
- She는 여성 한 사람을 나타내므로 복수형 teachers가 아닌 a teacher를 써야 합니다.

**It is a book.** 그것은 책이다.
- [It+be동사~] 다음에는 단수명사가 옵니다.

## 3 인칭대명사(주어)+be동사+장소를 나타내는 말

| 인칭대명사+be동사+ | at(in) the park<br>공원에 | He is at the park.<br>그는 공원에 있다. |
|---|---|---|
| | in the classroom<br>교실에 | We are in the classroom.<br>우리는 교실에 있다. |
| | at home<br>집에 | I am at home.<br>나는 집에 있다. |

# Warm Up

정답 및 해설 p. 4

## 1 다음 우리말과 일치하도록 괄호 안에서 알맞은 것을 고르세요.

01 He is ( a teacher / teachers ).
그는 선생님이다.

02 You are ( an actor / actors ).
너는 배우다.

03 We are ( cook / cooks ).
우리는 요리사들이다.

04 They are ( a flower / flowers ).
그것들은 꽃들이다.

05 It is ( a horse / horses ).
그것은 말이다.

06 She is in the ( room / classroom ).
그녀는 방에 있다.

07 They are ( cat / cats ).
그것들은 고양이들이다.

08 They are in the ( park / parking lot ).
그들은 공원에 있다.

09 She is ( a cook / cooks ).
그녀는 요리사다.

10 We are ( a movie star / movie stars ).
우리는 영화 배우들이다.

**Words**

□ actor 배우 □ cook 요리사 □ horse 말 □ classroom 교실 □ parking lot 주차장
□ movie star 영화 배우

## 1 다음 괄호 안에서 알맞은 것을 고르세요.

01 ( I am / You are ) doctors. 너희들은 의사들이다.

02 ( It is / They are ) doctors. 그들은 의사들이다.

03 ( She is / It is ) a book. 그것은 책이다.

04 ( He is / You are ) students. 너희들은 학생들이다.

05 ( We are / He is ) actors. 우리는 배우들이다.

06 ( It is / They are ) a tomato. 그것은 토마토다.

07 ( It is / They are ) snakes. 그것들은 뱀들이다.

08 ( He is / They are ) a cook. 그는 요리사다.

09 ( It is / We are ) a computer. 그것은 컴퓨터다.

10 ( You are / He is ) a student. 그는 학생이다.

11 ( He is / We are ) a taxi driver. 그는 택시 운전사다.

12 ( It is / We are ) taxi drivers. 우리는 택시 운전사들이다.

정답 및 해설 p. 4

## 2 다음 밑줄 친 부분을 바르게 고쳐 쓰세요.

01 We are dancer. → dancers
우리는 무용수들이다.

02 It is pencil. → ____________
그것은 연필이다.

03 She is teachers. → ____________
그녀는 선생님이다.

04 They are a watch. → ____________
그것들은 (손목)시계들이다.

05 I'm students. → ____________
나는 학생이다.

06 They are an apple. → ____________
그것들은 사과들이다.

07 She's singers. → ____________
그녀는 가수다.

08 We are friend. → ____________
우리는 친구들이다.

09 I'm doctor. → ____________
나는 의사다.

10 They are tree. → ____________
그것들은 나무들이다.

**Words**
☐ dancer 무용수 ☐ pencil 연필 ☐ watch (손목)시계 ☐ friend 친구 ☐ doctor 의사

## 1 다음 영어를 우리말로 쓰세요.

01 He is a teacher.

→ 그는 ___선생님이다___.

02 You are a student.

→ 너는 ______________.

03 We are doctors.

→ 우리는 ______________.

04 I'm a nurse.

→ 나는 ______________.

05 It is a horse.

→ 그것은 ______________.

06 She is in the room.

→ 그녀는 ______________.

07 They are bananas.

→ 그것들은 ______________.

08 They are in the park.

→ 그들은 ______________.

09 She is a cook.

→ 그녀는 ______________.

10 We are pilots.

→ 우리는 ______________.

**Words**

☐ nurse 간호사 ☐ horse 말 ☐ in the room 방에 ☐ banana 바나나
☐ in the park 공원에 ☐ pilot 비행기 조종사

## 2 다음 영어를 우리말로 쓰세요.

01 You are a police officer.
→ 너는 ____경찰관이다____.

02 I'm at home.
→ 나는 ________.

03 We are at the restaurant.
→ 우리는 ________.

04 They are in Korea.
→ 그들은 ________.

05 It is a pizza.
→ 그것은 ________.

06 They are carrots.
→ 그것들은 ________.

07 They are trees.
→ 그것들은 ________.

08 He is in the kitchen.
→ 그는 ________.

09 She is a painter.
→ 그녀는 ________.

10 It is a bird.
→ 그것은 ________.

**Words**

□ police officer 경찰관 □ at home 집에 □ restaurant 식당 □ carrot 당근
□ in the kitchen 부엌에 □ painter 화가 □ bird 새

## 1 다음 주어진 단어를 배열하여 우리말과 일치하도록 쓰세요.

01 그녀는 간호사다. (She / a nurse / is)

➡ She is a nurse.

02 그는 교실에 있다. (He / in the classroom / is)

➡ ______________________

03 그것은 컴퓨터다. (It / a computer / is)

➡ ______________________

04 우리는 거실에 있다. (are / We / in the living room)

➡ ______________________

05 그것들은 장미들이다. (roses / They / are)

➡ ______________________

06 그는 택시 운전사다. (a taxi driver / He / is)

➡ ______________________

07 그것은 수박이다. (It / a watermelon / is)

➡ ______________________

08 우리는 요리사들이다. (cooks / are / We)

➡ ______________________

09 나는 학생이다. (am / a student / I)

➡ ______________________

10 그는 선생님이다. (is / a teacher / He)

➡ ______________________

**Words**

☐ nurse 간호사 ☐ classroom 교실 ☐ living room 거실 ☐ driver 운전사
☐ watermelon 수박 ☐ cook 요리사

## 2 다음 주어진 단어를 이용하여 우리말을 영어로 쓰세요. (a 또는 an이 필요하면 쓰세요.)

01 우리는 학생들이다. (students)

➡ We are students.

02 그것은 악어다. (alligator)

➡ ______________________

03 그녀는 요리사다. (cook)

➡ ______________________

04 그것들은 자들이다. (rulers)

➡ ______________________

05 나는 화가다. (painter)

➡ ______________________

06 그것들은 곰들이다. (bears)

➡ ______________________

07 그는 배우다. (actor)

➡ ______________________

08 우리는 야구 선수들이다. (baseball players)

➡ ______________________

09 그녀는 선생님이다. (teacher)

➡ ______________________

10 그것들은 펭귄들이다. (penguins)

➡ ______________________

**Words**

□ alligator 악어 □ ruler 자 □ painter 화가 □ bear 곰 □ baseball player 야구 선수
□ penguin 펭귄

[1-2] 다음 중 빈칸에 공통으로 들어갈 알맞은 말을 고르세요.

**1**

그것들은 나뭇잎들이다.
→ ____________ are leaves.

그들은 내 사촌들이다.
→ ____________ are my cousins.

① I　② We　③ She
④ He　⑤ They

**2**

너는 학생이다.
→ You ____________ a student.

우리는 화가들이다.
→ We ____________ painters.

① be　② is　③ are
④ being　⑤ am

[3-4] 다음 중 잘못된 문장을 고르세요.

**3**

① I'm a pilot.
② He is a teacher.
③ She is in the classroom.
④ They are a computer.
⑤ It is a cat.

1.
**leaf** 나뭇잎
**cousin** 사촌

2.
be동사 are는 we, you, they와 함께 쓸 수 있습니다.

3.
they는 복수명사와 함께 씁니다.

## 4

① She is a dentist.

② We are scientists.

③ He is soccer players.

④ I'm a violinist.

⑤ You are dancers.

## 5

다음 밑줄 친 부분을 바르게 고쳐 쓰세요.

(1) We are doctor. → ________

(2) I'm soldier. → ________

(3) It is horses. → ________

(4) They are a bananas. → ________

(5) He is teachers. → ________

## 6

다음 영어를 우리말로 쓰세요.

(1) They are bears.

→ ____________________

(2) She is a singer.

→ ____________________

(3) We are at the museum.

→ ____________________

4.
He는 단수(한 사람)이므로 단수명사와 함께 합니다.

5.
**soldier** 군인
**horse** 말

6.
**museum** 박물관

다음 단어의 뜻을 쓰고, 단어를 더 써보세요.

| | | | | | | | |
|---|---|---|---|---|---|---|---|
| 01 | actor | 배우 | actor | 02 | alligator | | |
| 03 | animal | | | 04 | baseball | | |
| 05 | bear | | | 06 | bicycle | | |
| 07 | bird | | | 08 | calendar | | |
| 09 | carrot | | | 10 | classmate | | |
| 11 | classroom | | | 12 | cook | | |
| 13 | cousin | | | 14 | delicious | | |
| 15 | driver | | | 16 | elephant | | |
| 17 | friend | | | 18 | horse | | |
| 19 | king | | | 20 | kitchen | | |
| 21 | lawyer | | | 22 | movie | | |
| 23 | nurse | | | 24 | penguin | | |
| 25 | pilot | | | 26 | restaurant | | |
| 27 | room | | | 28 | singer | | |
| 29 | snake | | | 30 | tomato | | |

# CHAPTER 3
# 형용사

# 형용사의 종류

## 1 형용사의 종류

형용사란 명사의 모양이나 성질, 색깔, 크기 등을 설명해 주는 말입니다.

| | | | |
|---|---|---|---|
| 겉모습을 나타내는 형용사 | beautiful 아름다운<br>old 낡은, 오래된 | ugly 못생긴<br>young 어린, 젊은 | clean 깨끗한<br>dirty 더러운 |
| 색을 나타내는 형용사 | green 녹색의<br>black 검은, 검은색의<br>brown 갈색의 | blue 파란, 파란색의<br>red 빨간, 빨간색의<br>white 하얀, 하얀색의 | yellow 노란, 노란색의<br>pink 분홍색의 |
| 크기나 모양을 나타내는 형용사 | big 큰<br>long (길이 · 거리가) 긴 | small 작은<br>short 짧은 | tall 키가 큰, 높은<br>round 둥근 |
| 기분이나 상태를 나타내는 형용사 | happy 행복한<br>tired 피곤한 | sad 슬픈<br>angry 화가 난 | hungry 배고픈<br>sleepy 졸린 |

## 2 be동사+형용사

[주어+be동사+형용사]에서는 형용사가 주어를 보충 설명해 줍니다.

- He is **hungry.** 그는 배가 고프다. (He = hungry)
- The bus is **yellow.** 그 버스는 노란색이다. (The bus = yellow)

## 3 be동사+형용사+명사

형용사가 명사 앞에 와서 명사를 좀 더 자세히 설명해 줍니다.

- It is a **big dog.** 그것은 커다란 개다.
- It is a **black car.** 그것은 검은 자동차다.

**TIPS**
- 형용사 다음에 명사가 단수일 경우에는 형용사 앞에 a/an을 씁니다.
  **a big house** (커다란 집) / **an old bag** (낡은 가방)
- 형용사 다음에 명사가 복수일 경우에는 형용사 앞에 a/an을 쓸 수 없습니다.
  **~~a~~ big houses** (커다란 집들) / **~~an~~ old bags** (낡은 가방들)

# Warm Up

정답 및 해설 p. 5

## 1 다음 밑줄 친 단어가 형용사이면 O표, 명사이면 X표 하세요.

01 I'm <u>hungry</u>. → O
나는 배가 고프다.

02 It's an <u>old</u> car. → ______
그것은 낡은 자동차다.

03 She's a strong <u>girl</u>. → ______
그녀는 강한 소녀다.

04 This is a <u>round</u> table. → ______
이것은 둥근 식탁이다.

05 The dog is <u>small</u>. → ______
그 개는 작다.

06 It's a yellow <u>bus</u>. → ______
그것은 노란 버스다.

07 It's a <u>beautiful</u> bird. → ______
그것은 아름다운 새다.

08 The apple is <u>red</u>. → ______
그 사과는 빨간색이다.

09 He's a <u>tall</u> boy. → ______
그는 키가 큰 소년이다.

10 The room is <u>clean</u>. → ______
그 방은 깨끗하다.

**Words**

□ hungry 배고픈 □ old 낡은 □ strong 강한 □ round 둥근 □ yellow 노란
□ bus 버스 □ beautiful 아름다운 □ bird 새 □ clean 깨끗한

## 1 다음 형용사의 뜻을 쓰세요.

| | | | |
|---|---|---|---|
| 01 short → | 짧은 | 02 ugly → | ________ |
| 03 clean → | ________ | 04 round → | ________ |
| 05 angry → | ________ | 06 tired → | ________ |
| 07 sleepy → | ________ | 08 tall → | ________ |
| 09 brown → | ________ | 10 green → | ________ |
| 11 young → | ________ | 12 dirty → | ________ |

## 2 다음 의미에 맞는 형용사를 쓰세요.

| | | | |
|---|---|---|---|
| 01 큰 → | big | 02 빨간 → | ________ |
| 03 슬픈 → | ________ | 04 파란 → | ________ |
| 05 잘생긴 → | ________ | 06 긴 → | ________ |
| 07 배고픈 → | ________ | 08 강한 → | ________ |
| 09 행복한 → | ________ | 10 검은 → | ________ |
| 11 낡은 → | ________ | 12 아름다운 → | ________ |

**Words**

- □ ugly 못생긴 □ angry 화가 난 □ tired 피곤한 □ dirty 더러운 □ long 긴
- □ strong 강한 □ happy 행복한 □ black 검은

정답 및 해설 p. 5

## 3 다음 영어를 우리말로 쓰세요.

01 a beautiful girl → 아름다운 소녀

02 an old house → ______

03 a dirty car → ______

04 a yellow chair → ______

05 a big hamburger → ______

06 a small dog → ______

07 a round table → ______

08 a red apple → ______

09 a black cat → ______

10 a hungry boy → ______

11 a sleepy baby → ______

12 a tall building → ______

**Words**

☐ girl 소녀 ☐ dirty 더러운 ☐ chair 의자 ☐ hamburger 햄버거 ☐ table 식탁
☐ hungry 배고픈 ☐ sleepy 졸린 ☐ baby 아기 ☐ tall 높은 ☐ building 건물

# 1 다음 주어진 단어를 올바르게 정렬하고, 그 뜻을 쓰세요.

| | | | | |
|---|---|---|---|---|
| 01 | a / sleepy / baby | → | a sleepy baby | 졸린 아기 |
| 02 | a / bag / white | → | | |
| 03 | small / a / house | → | | |
| 04 | a / lion / hungry | → | | |
| 05 | beautiful / woman / a | → | | |
| 06 | handsome / a / boy | → | | |
| 07 | a / turtle / slow | → | | |
| 08 | girl / happy / a | → | | |
| 09 | a / nice / car | → | | |
| 10 | bridge / a / long | → | | |
| 11 | brown / a / bird | → | | |
| 12 | kind / teacher / a | → | | |

**Words**

□ white 하얀 □ lion 사자 □ woman 여자 □ handsome 잘생긴 □ turtle 거북
□ slow 느린 □ nice 멋진 □ bridge 다리 □ brown 갈색의 □ kind 친절한

## 2 다음 우리말과 일치하도록 보기의 단어를 이용하여 빈칸에 알맞은 말을 쓰세요.

| | | | |
|---|---|---|---|
| sleepy 졸린 | fast 빠른 | yellow 노란(색의) | sad 슬픈 |
| green 녹색의 | dirty 더러운 | short 짧은 | clean 깨끗한 |

**01** The room is ______clean______.
그 방은 깨끗하다.

**02** The train is ____________________.
그 기차는 빠르다.

**03** His hair is ____________________.
그의 머리카락은 짧다.

**04** The boys are ____________________.
그 소년들은 슬프다.

**05** The tree is ____________________.
그 나무는 녹색이다.

**06** They are ____________________ shoes.
그것들은 더러운 신발들이다.

**07** It is a ____________________ ribbon.
그것은 노란 리본이다.

**08** Sam is ____________________ now.
샘은 지금 졸리다.

**Words**
□ fast 빠른 □ sad 슬픈 □ dirty 더러운 □ clean 깨끗한 □ room 방 □ train 기차
□ hair 머리카락 □ shoe 신발 □ ribbon 리본

# 반대 의미의 형용사

## 1 반대 의미의 형용사

| clean | 깨끗한 | dirty | 더러운 |
|---|---|---|---|
| hot | 뜨거운 | cold | 차가운 |
| tall | 키가 큰 | short | 키가 작은 |
| old | 오래된, 낡은 | new | 새로운 |
| long | 길이가 긴 | short | 짧은 |
| big | 큰 | small | 작은 |
| fast | 빠른 | slow | 느린 |
| beautiful | 아름다운 | ugly | 못생긴 |
| hungry | 배고픈 | full | 배부른 |
| rich | 부유한 | poor | 가난한 |
| strong | 강한 | weak | 약한 |
| heavy | 무거운 | light | 가벼운 |

## 2 [(a/an)+형용사+명사]와 [be동사+형용사]

| (a/an)+형용사+명사 | be동사+형용사 |
|---|---|
| It is a round table.<br>그것은 둥근 식탁이다. | The table is round.<br>그 식탁은 둥글다. |
| He is a strong boy.<br>그는 강한 소년이다. | The boy is strong.<br>그 소년은 강하다. |
| She is a beautiful girl.<br>그녀는 아름다운 소녀다. | The girl is beautiful.<br>그 소녀는 아름답다. |

# Warm Up

정답 및 해설 p. 5

## 1 다음 형용사의 반대말을 고르세요.

01 early 이른 → late / fast 늦은

02 beautiful 아름다운 → ugly / new 못생긴

03 hungry 배고픈 → small / full 배부른

04 big 큰 → small / poor 작은

05 clean 깨끗한 → long / dirty 더러운

06 rich 부유한 → poor / strong 가난한

07 strong 강한 → weak / long 약한

08 long 긴 → short / dirty 짧은

09 old 오래된, 낡은 → ugly / new 새로운

10 tall 키가 큰 → long / short 키가 작은

11 hot 뜨거운 → cold / slow 차가운

12 fast 빠른 → slow / clean 느린

### Words

☐ late 늦은 ☐ ugly 못생긴 ☐ full 배부른 ☐ poor 가난한 ☐ dirty 더러운
☐ strong 강한 ☐ weak 약한 ☐ short 짧은, 키가 작은 ☐ slow 느린

## 1 다음 보기의 단어를 이용하여 빈칸에 알맞은 말을 쓰세요.

| | | | | |
|---|---|---|---|---|
| old 낡은 | full 배부른 | hot 뜨거운 | new 새로운 | short 키가 작은 |
| fast 빠른 | slow 느린 | hungry 배고픈 | cold 차가운 | tall 키가 큰 |

01 The brown shoes are ____old____.
The pink shoes are __________.

02 She is __________.
He is __________.

03 The coffee is __________.
The orange juice is __________.

04 The man is __________.
The boy is __________.

05 The rabbit is __________.
The turtle is __________.

**Words**

□ full 배부른 □ new 새로운 □ short 키가 작은 □ shoe 신발 □ pink 분홍색의
□ coffee 커피 □ rabbit 토끼 □ turtle 거북

정답 및 해설 p. 5

## 2 다음 보기의 단어를 이용하여 빈칸에 알맞은 말을 쓰세요. (필요하면 be동사도 넣으세요.)

| | | | | |
|---|---|---|---|---|
| clean 깨끗한 | long 긴 | short 짧은 | small 작은 | sad 슬픈 |
| big 큰 | happy 행복한 | poor 가난한 | dirty 더러운 | rich 부유한 |

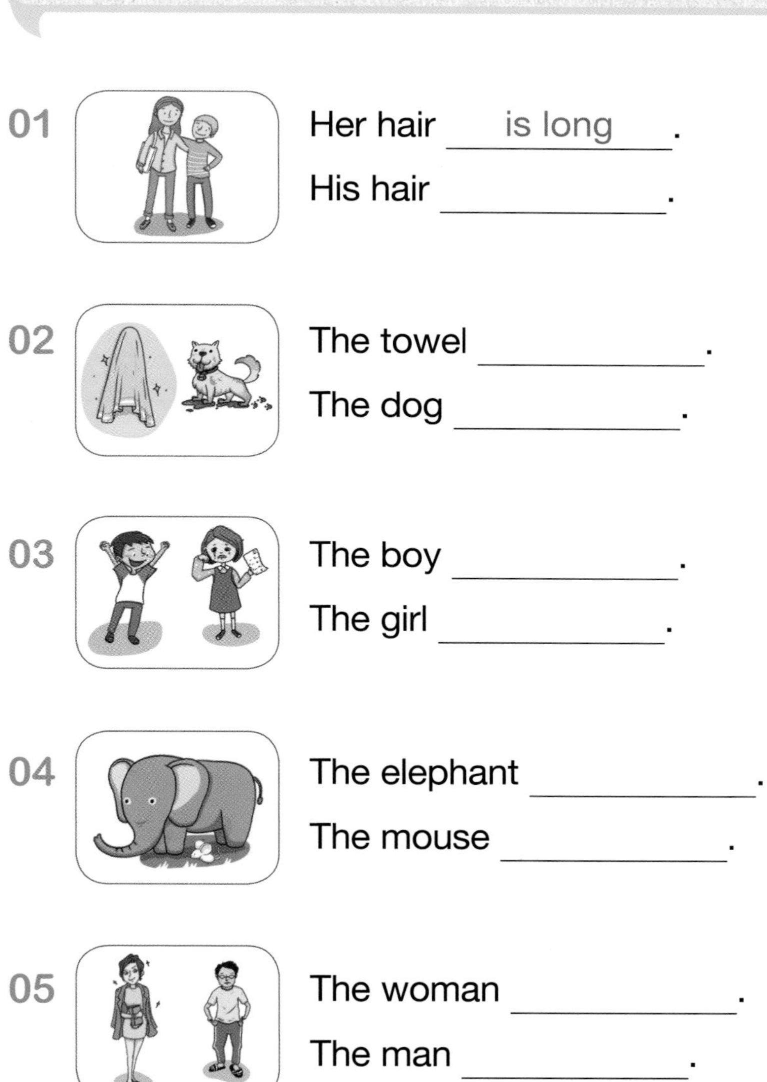

01 Her hair is long.
His hair ________.

02 The towel ________.
The dog ________.

03 The boy ________.
The girl ________.

04 The elephant ________.
The mouse ________.

05 The woman ________.
The man ________.

**Words**

☐ sad 슬픈 ☐ happy 행복한 ☐ poor 가난한 ☐ dirty 더러운 ☐ rich 부유한
☐ hair 머리카락 ☐ towel 수건 ☐ elephant 코끼리 ☐ mouse 쥐

## 1 다음 주어진 문장을 보기처럼 바꿔 쓰세요.

> It is a new bike. ➡ The bike is new.
> 그것은 새 자전거다. 그 자전거는 새것이다.

01 They are dirty shoes. ➡ The shoes ___are dirty___.
그것들은 더러운 신발들이다. 그 신발들은 더럽다.

02 It is a black ribbon. ➡ The ribbon ________________.
그것은 검은 리본이다. 그 리본은 검은색이다.

03 She is a rich woman. ➡ The woman ________________.
그녀는 부유한 여자다. 그 여자는 부유하다.

04 He is a poor boy. ➡ The boy ________________.
그는 가난한 소년이다. 그 소년은 가난하다.

05 It is a sad movie. ➡ The movie ________________.
그것은 슬픈 영화다. 그 영화는 슬프다.

06 It is a heavy box. ➡ The box ________________.
그것은 무거운 상자다. 그 상자는 무겁다.

07 It is an ugly dog. ➡ The dog ________________.
그것은 못생긴 개다. 그 개는 못생겼다.

08 They are tall trees. ➡ The trees ________________.
그것들은 키가 큰 나무들이다. 그 나무들은 키가 크다.

**Words**
□ dirty 더러운 □ ribbon 리본 □ rich 부유한 □ poor 가난한 □ sad 슬픈
□ movie 영화 □ heavy 무거운 □ ugly 못생긴 □ tree 나무

## 2 다음 주어진 문장을 보기처럼 바꿔 쓰세요.

The bike is new. → It is a new bike.
그 자전거는 새것이다. 그것은 새 자전거다.

01 The watch is old. → It is an old watch.
그 (손목)시계는 낡았다. 그것은 낡은 (손목)시계다.

02 The boys are smart. → They are ______________.
그 소년들은 영리하다. 그들은 영리한 소년들이다.

03 The man is brave. → He is a ______________.
그 남자는 용감하다. 그는 용감한 남자다.

04 The bag is brown. → It is a ______________.
그 가방은 갈색이다. 그것은 갈색 가방이다.

05 The chair is yellow. → It is a ______________.
그 의자는 노란색이다. 그것은 노란 의자다.

06 The boy is weak. → He is a ______________.
그 소년은 약하다. 그는 약한 소년이다.

07 The buildings are tall. → They are ______________.
그 건물들은 높다. 그것들은 높은 건물들이다.

08 The table is round. → It is a ______________.
그 식탁은 둥글다. 그것은 둥근 식탁이다.

**Words**
□ brave 용감한 □ color 색깔 □ brown 갈색의 □ chair 의자 □ weak 약한
□ building 건물 □ table 식탁 □ round 둥근

## 1 다음 주어진 형용사를 이용하여 빈칸에 알맞은 말을 쓰세요.

01 그 자동차는 새것이다. (new)

➡ The car ___is___ ___new___.

02 그 학생은 영리하다. (smart)

➡ The student ______ ______.

03 그녀는 아름다운 소녀다. (beautiful)

➡ She is ______ ______ ______.

04 그것은 비싼 가방이다. (expensive)

➡ It is ______ ______ ______.

05 나는 빨간 사과를 가지고 있다. (red)

➡ I have ______ ______ ______.

06 그들은 부지런한 학생들이다. (diligent)

➡ They are ______ ______.

07 그는 용감하다. (brave)

➡ He ______ ______.

08 그녀는 강한 여자다. (strong)

➡ She is ______ ______ ______.

09 그 커피는 뜨겁다. (hot)

➡ The coffee ______ ______.

10 나는 배가 고프다. (hungry)

➡ I ______ ______.

**Words**

☐ new 새로운 ☐ smart 영리한 ☐ expensive 비싼 ☐ diligent 부지런한
☐ brave 용감한 ☐ strong 강한 ☐ coffee 커피 ☐ hungry 배고픈

## 2 다음 문장이 반대 의미가 되도록 빈칸에 알맞은 말을 쓰세요.

01 The car is old. 그 자동차는 낡았다.
➡ The car ___is___ ___new___. 그 자동차는 새것이다.

02 She is rich. 그녀는 부자다.
➡ She ______ ______. 그녀는 가난하다.

03 He is a strong boy. 그는 강한 소년이다.
➡ He is ______ ______ ______. 그는 약한 소년이다.

04 The train is slow. 그 기차는 느리다.
➡ The train ______ ______. 그 기차는 빠르다.

05 The girls are tall. 그 소녀들은 키가 크다.
➡ The girls ______ ______. 그 소녀들은 키가 작다.

06 The box is heavy. 그 상자는 무겁다.
➡ The box ______ ______. 그 상자는 가볍다.

07 The water is hot. 그 물은 뜨겁다.
➡ The water ______ ______. 그 물은 차갑다.

08 They are hungry. 그들은 배가 고프다.
➡ They ______ ______. 그들은 배가 부르다.

09 The house is big. 그 집은 크다.
➡ The house ______ ______. 그 집은 작다.

10 It is a short bridge. 그것은 짧은 다리다.
➡ It is ______ ______ ______. 그것은 긴 다리다.

**Words**

☐ rich 부유한 ☐ strong 강한 ☐ train 기차 ☐ slow 느린 ☐ box 상자
☐ heavy 무거운 ☐ water 물 ☐ bridge 다리

[1-2] 다음 중 형용사가 아닌 것을 고르세요.

**1**

① pretty ② big
③ school ④ rich
⑤ young

**2**

① beautiful ② old
③ happy ④ strong
⑤ picture

**3** 다음 중 반대말끼리 짝지어지지 않은 것을 고르세요.

① fast – slow
② long – short
③ round – square
④ strong – weak
⑤ hot – cold

**4** 다음 중 그림을 보고 빈칸에 들어갈 말을 고르세요.

The shoes are __________.

① rich ② old ③ happy
④ strong ⑤ short

1.
명사와 형용사를 구분해 보세요.
**school** 학교

2.
**picture** 사진

3.
모양을 나타내는 단어를 찾아보세요.
**round** 둥근
**square** 정사각형의
**hot** 뜨거운
**cold** 차가운

**5** 다음 형용사의 반대말을 쓰세요.

(1) **beautiful** ➡ ____________

(2) **big** ➡ ____________

(3) **clean** ➡ ____________

(4) **new** ➡ ____________

(5) **poor** ➡ ____________

**6** 다음 보기처럼 문장을 바꿔 쓰세요.

He is a tall boy. ➜ The boy is tall.

(1) It is a long bridge.

➡ ______________________________

(2) She is a smart girl.

➡ ______________________________

(3) It is a fast horse.

➡ ______________________________

6.
**smart** 영리한
**horse** 말

**7** 다음 우리말과 일치하도록 빈칸에 알맞은 말을 쓰세요.

(1) 그는 키가 작다.

➡ He ______________________________.

(2) 그들은 배가 고프다.

➡ They ______________________________.

다음 단어의 뜻을 쓰고, 단어를 더 써보세요.

| | | | | | | | |
|---|---|---|---|---|---|---|---|
| 01 | angry | 화가 난 | angry | 02 | baby | | |
| 03 | beautiful | | | 04 | box | | |
| 05 | brave | | | 06 | bridge | | |
| 07 | brown | | | 08 | building | | |
| 09 | bus | | | 10 | dirty | | |
| 11 | green | | | 12 | hair | | |
| 13 | handsome | | | 14 | hungry | | |
| 15 | late | | | 16 | long | | |
| 17 | nice | | | 18 | picture | | |
| 19 | poor | | | 20 | ribbon | | |
| 21 | rich | | | 22 | round | | |
| 23 | sleepy | | | 24 | slow | | |
| 25 | square | | | 26 | strong | | |
| 27 | tired | | | 28 | ugly | | |
| 29 | weak | | | 30 | white | | |

# CHAPTER 4
# be동사의 부정문과 의문문

# be동사의 부정문

## 1 부정문

1 부정문이란 '~ 하지 않다', '~이 아니다'라는 부정의 의미를 나타내는 문장을 말합니다.

2 be동사가 있는 문장에서는 be동사 다음에 not을 붙여 부정문을 만듭니다.

## 2 주어가 단수일 때 부정문 만들기

| 긍정문 | 부정문 |
|---|---|
| I am a doctor. | I **am not** a doctor. 나는 의사가 아니다. |
| You are a student. | You **are not** a student. 너는 학생이 아니다. |
| She is smart. | She **is not** smart. 그녀는 영리하지 않다. |
| He is strong. | He **is not** strong. 그는 강하지 않다. |
| It is a book. | It **is not** a book. 그것은 책이 아니다. |
| The car is new. | The car **is not** new. 그 자동차는 새것이 아니다. |

## 3 주어가 복수일 때 부정문 만들기

| 긍정문 | 부정문 |
|---|---|
| We are doctors. | We **are not** doctors. 우리는 의사들이 아니다. |
| You are students. | You **are not** students. 너희들은 학생들이 아니다. |
| They are smart. | They **are not** smart. 그들은 영리하지 않다. |
| They are books. | They **are not** books. 그것들은 책들이 아니다. |
| The cars are new. | The cars **are not** new. 그 자동차들은 새것이 아니다. |

## 4 be동사의 부정문 축약

부정문을 다음과 같이 줄여서 사용할 수 있습니다.

| | | |
|---|---|---|
| I am not ~. | → | **I'm not** ~. |
| She/He/It is not ~. | → | She/He/It **isn't** ~. |
| We/You /They are not ~. | → | We/You/They **aren't** ~. |

# Warm Up

정답 및 해설 p. 6

## 1 다음 우리말과 일치하도록 괄호 안에서 알맞은 것을 고르세요.

**01** We ( are / are not ) tourists.
우리는 관광객들이 아니다.

**02** He ( is / is not ) happy.
그는 행복하다.

**03** It ( is / is not ) a penguin.
그것은 펭귄이 아니다.

**04** The magazines ( are / are not ) expensive.
그 잡지들은 비싸지 않다.

**05** They ( are / are not ) my cousins.
그들은 나의 사촌들이다.

**06** She ( is / isn't ) kind.
그녀는 친절하지 않다.

**07** I ( am / am not ) a lawyer.
나는 변호사가 아니다.

**08** They ( are / aren't ) painters.
그들은 화가들이다.

**09** The box ( is / isn't ) heavy.
그 상자는 무겁지 않다.

**10** It ( is / isn't ) a computer.
그것은 컴퓨터다.

### Words

□ tourist 관광객 □ penguin 펭귄 □ magazine 잡지 □ expensive 비싼
□ cousin 사촌 □ lawyer 변호사 □ painter 화가 □ heavy 무거운

## 1 다음 문장을 부정문으로 바꿔 쓰세요. (축약형을 쓰지 마세요.)

01 They are zebras. 그것들은 얼룩말들이다.

→ They are not zebras.

02 You are weak. 너는 약하다.

→ ______________________

03 She is a writer. 그녀는 작가다.

→ ______________________

04 He is a baseball player. 그는 야구 선수다.

→ ______________________

05 The bike is new. 그 자전거는 새것이다.

→ ______________________

06 The apples are fresh. 그 사과들은 신선하다.

→ ______________________

07 The spaghetti is delicious. 그 스파게티는 맛있다.

→ ______________________

08 They are politicians. 그들은 정치가들이다.

→ ______________________

09 The house is big. 그 집은 크다.

→ ______________________

10 The dogs are fast. 그 개들은 빠르다.

→ ______________________

**Words**

□ zebra 얼룩말 □ weak 약한 □ writer 작가 □ baseball player 야구 선수
□ fresh 신선한 □ spaghetti 스파게티 □ delicious 맛있는 □ politician 정치가

## 2 다음 문장을 부정문으로 바꿔 쓰세요. (축약형으로 만드세요.)

01 He is a taxi driver. 그는 택시 운전사다.

➡ He isn't a taxi driver.

02 She is hungry. 그녀는 배가 고프다.

➡ ______________________

03 They are pumpkins. 그것들은 호박들이다.

➡ ______________________

04 The book is interesting. 그 책은 재미있다.

➡ ______________________

05 I'm a dancer. 나는 무용수다.

➡ ______________________

06 It is a stone. 그것은 돌이다.

➡ ______________________

07 We are English teachers. 우리는 영어 선생님들이다.

➡ ______________________

08 The girls are very tall. 그 소녀들은 매우 키가 크다.

➡ ______________________

09 The man is handsome. 그 남자는 잘생겼다.

➡ ______________________

10 You are a pianist. 너는 피아니스트다.

➡ ______________________

**Words**

- ☐ driver 운전사
- ☐ pumpkin 호박
- ☐ interesting 재미있는
- ☐ dancer 무용수
- ☐ stone 돌
- ☐ handsome 잘생긴
- ☐ pianist 피아니스트

# 1 다음 주어진 단어를 이용하여 빈칸에 알맞은 말을 쓰세요.

**01** 그들은 의사들이 아니다. 그들은 간호사들이다. (doctors / nurses)

➡ They aren't doctors . They are nurses .

**02** 그것은 상어가 아니다. 그것은 고래다. (a shark / a whale)

➡ It ______________ . It ______________ .

**03** 나는 무용수가 아니다. 나는 배우다. (a dancer / an actor)

➡ I ______________ . I ______________ .

**04** 우리는 선생님들이 아니다. 우리는 학생들이다. (teachers / students)

➡ We ______________ . We ______________ .

**05** 그것들은 호랑이들이 아니다. 그것들은 사자들이다. (tigers / lions)

➡ They ______________ . They ______________ .

**06** 그녀는 왕이 아니다. 그녀는 여왕이다. (a king / a queen)

➡ She ______________ . She ______________ .

**07** 그는 배가 고프지 않다. 그는 배가 부르다. (hungry / full)

➡ He ______________ . He ______________ .

**08** 우리는 슬프지 않다. 우리는 행복하다. (sad / happy)

➡ We ______________ . We ______________ .

**09** 그것은 장미가 아니다. 그것은 카네이션이다. (a rose / a carnation)

➡ It ______________ . It ______________ .

**10** 너는 뚱뚱하지 않다. 너는 날씬하다. (fat / slim)

➡ You ______________ . You ______________ .

**Words**

□ doctor 의사 □ nurse 간호사 □ shark 상어 □ whale 고래 □ dancer 무용수
□ king 왕 □ queen 여왕 □ rose 장미 □ carnation 카네이션 □ fat 뚱뚱한

## 2 다음 주어진 단어를 이용하여 빈칸에 알맞은 말을 쓰세요. (필요하면 a나 an을 넣으세요.)

01 그것들은 사과들이 아니다. 그것들은 오렌지들이다. (apples / oranges)

➡ They aren't apples. They are oranges.

02 그는 웨이터가 아니다. 그는 요리사다. (waiter / cook)

➡ He ______________. He ______________.

03 그 자동차는 오래되지 않았다. 그 자동차는 새것이다. (old / new)

➡ The car ______________. The car ______________.

04 그것은 새가 아니다. 그것은 곤충이다. (bird / insect)

➡ It ______________. It ______________.

05 그는 도둑이 아니다. 그는 경찰이다. (thief / police officer)

➡ He ______________. He ______________.

06 그것은 기린이 아니다. 그것은 얼룩말이다. (giraffe / zebra)

➡ It ______________. It ______________.

07 그것들은 양말들이 아니다. 그것들은 신발들이다. (socks / shoes)

➡ They ______________. They ______________.

08 그는 못생기지 않았다. 그는 잘생겼다. (ugly / handsome)

➡ He ______________. He ______________.

09 그 신발들은 깨끗하지 않다. 그 신발들은 더럽다. (clean / dirty)

➡ The shoes ______________. The shoes ______________.

10 그 남자는 부자가 아니다. 그 남자는 가난하다. (rich / poor)

➡ The man ______________. The man ______________.

**Words**

- ☐ orange 오렌지
- ☐ waiter 웨이터
- ☐ cook 요리사
- ☐ insect 곤충
- ☐ thief 도둑
- ☐ police officer 경찰관
- ☐ giraffe 기린
- ☐ ugly 못생긴
- ☐ dirty 더러운

# be동사의 의문문

## be동사의 의문문 만들기

1 의문문이란 상대방에게 질문을 하는 문장을 말합니다.

2 be동사가 있는 문장을 의문문으로 만들려면 주어와 be동사의 위치를 바꾸고 문장 끝에 물음표(?)를 붙입니다.

| 긍정문 | 의문문 |
|---|---|
| You are a student. | **Are you** a student? 당신은 학생인가요? |
| She is a student. | **Is she** a student? 그녀는 학생인가요? |
| He is a student. | **Is he** a student? 그는 학생인가요? |
| It is a book. | **Is it** a book? 그것은 책인가요? |
| We are students. | **Are we** students? 우리는 학생들인가요? |
| You are students. | **Are you** students? 당신들은 학생들인가요? *you(복수) |
| They are students. | **Are they** students? 그들은 학생들인가요? |

## be동사가 있는 의문문 대답하기

be동사가 있는 의문문은 Yes나 No로 답해야 합니다.

| 의문문 | 대답 (긍정) | 대답 (부정) |
|---|---|---|
| Are you a student? | Yes, I am. | No, I am not. (No, I'm not.) |
| Is she a student? | Yes, she is. | No, she isn't. |
| Is he a student? | Yes, he is. | No, he isn't. |
| Is it a book? | Yes, it is. | No, it isn't. |
| Are we students? | Yes, you are. | No, you aren't. |
| Are you students? | Yes, we are. | No, we aren't. |
| Are they students? | Yes, they are. | No, they aren't. |

TIPS Is the boy a student?으로 질문했을 때에는 Yes, the boy is.나 No, the boy isn't.가 아니고 Yes, **he is**.나 No, **he isn't**.로 대답합니다. (the boy = he)

예 Is **the girl** a student? 그 소녀는 학생인가요? Yes, **she is**. / No, **she isn't**. (the girl = she)

정답 및 해설 p. 7

## 1 다음 문장을 의문문으로 바꿔 쓰세요.

01 You are tall. 너는 키가 크다.

➡ Are you tall?

02 She is Chinese. 그녀는 중국인이다.

➡ ____________ Chinese?

03 It is a ruler. 그것은 자다.

➡ ____________ a ruler?

04 They are soldiers. 그들은 군인들이다.

➡ ____________ soldiers?

05 The man is a firefighter. 그 남자는 소방관이다.

➡ ____________ a firefighter?

06 He is sleepy. 그는 졸리다.

➡ ____________ sleepy?

07 They are turtles. 그것들은 거북들이다.

➡ ____________ turtles?

08 We are movie stars. 우리는 영화 배우들이다.

➡ ____________ movie stars?

09 Mike is a student. 마이크는 학생이다.

➡ ____________ a student?

10 They are at the park. 그들은 공원에 있다

➡ ____________ at the park?

**Words**

☐ Chinese 중국인(의) ☐ ruler 자 ☐ soldier 군인 ☐ firefighter 소방관 ☐ turtle 거북
☐ movie star 영화 배우 ☐ at the park 공원에

## 1 다음 그림을 보고 질문에 알맞은 답변을 쓰세요.

01
A: Is he a doctor? 그는 의사인가요?
B: Yes, he is . 예, 그래요.

02
A: Is it a lion? 그것은 사자인가요?
B: No, ______________. 아니요, 그렇지 않아요.

03
A: Is it a cucumber? 그것은 오이인가요?
B: No, ______________. 아니요, 그렇지 않아요.

04
A: Are we police officers? 우리는 경찰관들인가요?
B: Yes, ______________. 예, 그래요.

05
A: Are you cooks? 당신들은 요리사들인가요?
B: Yes, ______________. 예, 그래요.

06
A: Is the girl in the classroom? 그 소녀는 교실에 있나요?
B: No, ______________. 아니요, 그렇지 않아요.

07
A: Is he a scientist? 그는 과학자인가요?
B: No, ______________. 아니요, 그렇지 않아요.

08
A: Are they strawberries? 그것들은 딸기들인가요?
B: No, ______________. 아니요, 그렇지 않아요.

### Words

☐ cucumber 오이 ☐ police officer 경찰관 ☐ cook 요리사 ☐ classroom 교실
☐ scientist 과학자 ☐ strawberry 딸기

## 2 다음 그림을 보고 질문에 알맞은 답변을 쓰세요.

01 A: Is he a painter? 그는 화가인가요?
B: No, ___he isn't___. 아니요, 그렇지 않아요.

02 A: Is it an eraser? 그것은 지우개인가요?
B: No, ______________. 아니요, 그렇지 않아요.

03 A: Are you a vet? 당신은 수의사인가요?
B: Yes, ______________. 예, 그래요.

04 A: Are they gummy candies? 그것들은 젤리들인가요?
B: Yes, ______________. 예, 그래요.

05 A: Is the woman a doctor? 그 여자는 의사인가요?
B: No, ______________. 아니요, 그렇지 않아요.

06 A: Is the man a golfer? 그 남자는 골프 선수인가요?
B: Yes, ______________. 예, 그래요.

07 A: Is it a pumpkin? 그것은 호박인가요?
B: No, ______________. 아니요, 그렇지 않아요.

08 A: Is the boy in the room? 그 소년은 방에 있나요?
B: Yes, ______________. 예, 그래요.

**Words**

- ☐ painter 화가
- ☐ eraser 지우개
- ☐ vet 수의사
- ☐ golfer 골프 선수
- ☐ pumpkin 호박
- ☐ in the room 방에

# 1 다음 빈칸에 알맞은 말을 쓰세요.

01 A: Is she a doctor? 그녀는 의사인가요?
B: Yes, ___she___ ___is___.

02 A: ________ ________ a baker? 당신은 제빵사인가요?
B: No, I'm not.

03 A: Are the vegetables fresh? 그 야채들은 신선한가요?
B: Yes, ________ ________.

04 A: Is the boy a singer? 그 소년은 가수인가요?
B: Yes, ________ ________.

05 A: Is the girl diligent? 그 소녀는 부지런한가요?
B: Yes, ________ ________.

06 A: Is the woman sick? 그 여자는 아픈가요?
B: No, ________ ________.

07 A: Are the students in the classroom? 그 학생들은 교실에 있나요?
B: No, ________ ________.

08 A: Is it a pencil? 그것은 연필인가요?
B: Yes, ________ ________.

09 A: Are you students? 당신들은 학생들인가요?
B: No, ________ ________.

10 A: Are you tired? 당신은 피곤한가요?
B: No, ________ ________.

**Words**
- □ baker 제빵사 □ vegetable 야채 □ fresh 신선한 □ singer 가수 □ diligent 부지런한
- □ sick 아픈 □ classroom 교실 □ tired 피곤한

정답 및 해설 p. 7

## 2 다음 문장을 주어진 지시대로 바꿔 쓰세요.

01 I'm hungry. 나는 배가 고프다.
➡ 부정문 I'm not hungry.

02 She is a lawyer. 그녀는 변호사다.
➡ 의문문 ______

03 We are famous singers. 우리들은 유명한 가수들이다.
➡ 부정문 ______

04 He is a soccer player. 그는 축구 선수다.
➡ 의문문 ______

05 Jane is a nurse. 제인은 간호사다.
➡ 의문문 ______

06 The box is heavy. 그 상자는 무겁다.
➡ 부정문 ______

07 She is in the classroom. 그녀는 교실에 있다.
➡ 부정문 ______

08 They are diligent students. 그들은 부지런한 학생들이다.
➡ 의문문 ______

09 He is in the library. 그는 도서관에 있다.
➡ 의문문 ______

10 They are fresh vegetables. 그것들은 신선한 야채들이다.
➡ 부정문 ______

**Words**

□ lawyer 변호사 □ famous 유명한 □ soccer 축구 □ nurse 간호사 □ heavy 무거운
□ diligent 부지런한 □ library 도서관 □ fresh 신선한 □ vegetable 야채

# 1 다음 문장을 부정문과 의문문으로 바꿔 쓰세요.

01 You are happy. 너는 행복하다.

부정문 You aren't happy.

의문문 Are you happy?

02 She is Korean. 그녀는 한국인이다.

부정문 ____________________

의문문 ____________________

03 It is a camera. 그것은 카메라다.

부정문 ____________________

의문문 ____________________

04 They are cooks. 그들은 요리사들이다.

부정문 ____________________

의문문 ____________________

05 You are firefighters. 너희들은 소방관들이다.

부정문 ____________________

의문문 ____________________

06 We are police officers. 우리는 경찰관들이다.

부정문 ____________________

의문문 ____________________

07 He is in the room. 그는 방에 있다.

부정문 ____________________

의문문 ____________________

**Words**

□ Korean 한국인(의) □ camera 카메라 □ cook 요리사 □ firefighter 소방관
□ police officer 경찰관 □ in the room 방에

## 2 다음 밑줄 친 부분을 바르게 고쳐 쓰세요.

01 A: Are you a doctor? ➡ Is she a doctor? 그녀는 의사인가요?
B: Yes, she is.

02 A: Are we a baker? ➡ ______ ______ a baker? 당신은 제빵사인가요?
B: No, I'm not.

03 A: Is it fresh? ➡ ______ ______ fresh? 그것들은 신선한가요?
B: Yes, they are.

04 A: Are you a boxer? ➡ ______ ______ a boxer? 그는 권투선수인가요?
B: Yes, he is.

05 A: Are you nurses? ➡ ______ ______ nurses? 그들은 간호사들인가요?
B: Yes, they are.

06 A: Is the girl sick? 그 소녀는 아픈가요?
B: No, he isn't. ➡ No, ______ ______.

07 A: Are you a pilot? 당신은 비행기 조종사인가요?
B: Yes, he is. ➡ Yes, ______ ______.

08 A: Is the boy diligent? 그 소년은 부지런한가요?
B: Yes, they are. ➡ Yes, ______ ______.

09 A: Are you students? 당신들은 학생들인가요?
B: Yes, I am. ➡ Yes, ______ ______.

10 A: Is it a book? 그것은 책인가요?
B: No, he isn't. ➡ No, ______ ______.

**Words**

☐ doctor 의사 ☐ baker 제빵사 ☐ fresh 신선한 ☐ boxer 권투선수 ☐ nurse 간호사
☐ sick 아픈 ☐ pilot 비행기 조종사 ☐ diligent 부지런한

# Exercise CHAPTER 4

[1-2] 다음 중 대화의 빈칸에 들어갈 알맞은 대답을 고르세요.

**1**

A: Are you doctors?
B: Yes, ______________________.

① I am ② he is ③ she is
④ they are ⑤ we are

**2**

A: Is the man diligent?
B: Yes, ______________________.

① I am ② he is ③ she is
④ they are ⑤ we are

**3** 다음 중 잘못된 문장을 고르세요.

① I'm not an actor.
② He isn't a nurse.
③ Is it a carrot?
④ They isn't pianists.
⑤ Are you a writer?

**4** 다음 중 우리말과 일치하도록 빈칸에 들어갈 말을 고르세요.

우리는 교실에 있지 않다.
➡ We ____________ in the classroom.

① am not ② is ③ is not
④ are ⑤ aren't

1.
you가 복수형이므로
대답은 we로 해야 합니다.

2.
the man은 he로 대답합니다.
**diligent** 부지런한

3.
**carrot** 당근
**pianist** 피아니스트

[5-6] 다음 그림을 보고 빈칸에 알맞은 말을 쓰세요.

**5**

He __________ a doctor.
He is a police officer.

**6**

They __________ bananas.
They are apples.

**7** 다음 문장을 부정문과 의문문으로 바꿔 쓰세요.

(1) Susan is a teacher.

부정문 ______________________________

의문문 ______________________________

(2) The vegetables are fresh.

부정문 ______________________________

의문문 ______________________________

(3) They are smart students.

부정문 ______________________________

의문문 ______________________________

7.
**fresh** 신선한
**smart** 영리한

**8** 다음 대화의 빈칸에 알맞은 말을 쓰세요.

A: Is the girl tall?
B: Yes, __________.

➡ ______________________________

8.
**tall** 키가 큰

다음 단어의 뜻을 쓰고, 단어를 더 써보세요.

| No. | Word | 뜻 | 쓰기 | No. | Word | 뜻 | 쓰기 |
|---|---|---|---|---|---|---|---|
| 01 | boxer | 권투선수 | boxer | 02 | camera | | |
| 03 | cucumber | | | 04 | dancer | | |
| 05 | diligent | | | 06 | doctor | | |
| 07 | eraser | | | 08 | expensive | | |
| 09 | famous | | | 10 | fat | | |
| 11 | fresh | | | 12 | heavy | | |
| 13 | insect | | | 14 | library | | |
| 15 | magazine | | | 16 | painter | | |
| 17 | politician | | | 18 | pumpkin | | |
| 19 | scientist | | | 20 | shark | | |
| 21 | sick | | | 22 | slim | | |
| 23 | smart | | | 24 | soldier | | |
| 25 | thief | | | 26 | tourist | | |
| 27 | turtle | | | 28 | vet | | |
| 29 | whale | | | 30 | writer | | |

# CHAPTER 5
# 동사

# 일반동사

## 일반동사의 의미와 위치

1 일반동사란 우리가 하는 모든 행동이나 상태 등을 나타내는 말입니다.
예를 들어, '달리다', '먹다', '좋아하다', '사랑하다' 등이 있습니다.

2 일반동사의 위치
동사는 일반적으로 '주어' 다음에 위치해서 주어의 동작이나 상태를 설명해 줍니다.

I watch TV. 나는 TV를 본다.
(주어) (동사)

We go to school. 우리는 학교에 간다.
(주어) (동사)

## 동사의 활용

| | |
|---|---|
| I / You / They / We (나는 / 너는 / 그들은 / 우리는) | like apples. 사과를 좋아한다. |
| | watch TV. TV를 본다. |
| | go to school. 학교에 간다. |
| | study English. 영어를 공부한다. |
| | have a computer. 컴퓨터를 가지고 있다. |
| | eat pizza. 피자를 먹는다. |

# Warm Up

정답 및 해설 p. 8

## 1 다음 동사의 의미를 쓰세요.

01 eat → 먹다

02 go → ______

03 drink → ______

04 cry → ______

05 watch → ______

06 wash → ______

07 play → ______

08 have → ______

09 read → ______

10 work → ______

11 study → ______

12 do → ______

13 talk → ______

14 cook → ______

15 sleep → ______

16 stay → ______

17 run → ______

18 walk → ______

19 buy → ______

20 teach → ______

21 sing → ______

22 like → ______

23 learn → ______

24 visit → ______

☐ cry 울다 ☐ wash 씻다 ☐ study 공부하다 ☐ do 하다 ☐ talk 말하다
☐ sleep 잠자다 ☐ stay 머물다

## 1 다음 문장에서 동사에 동그라미 하고, 그 뜻을 쓰세요.

01 I (eat) dinner at seven. → 먹다
나는 7시에 저녁을 먹는다.

02 I read books. → ______
나는 책을 읽는다.

03 They cry at night. → ______
그들은 밤에 운다.

04 You play the piano. → ______
너는 피아노를 연주한다.

05 We like fruit. → ______
우리는 과일을 좋아한다.

06 We love music. → ______
우리는 음악을 사랑한다.

07 They sleep on the floor. → ______
그들은 바닥에서 잠을 잔다.

08 The dogs run fast. → ______
그 개들은 빨리 달린다.

09 They study at the library. → ______
그들은 도서관에서 공부한다.

10 I wash the dishes. → ______
나는 설거지를 한다.

11 We talk on the phone. → ______
우리는 전화로 말한다.

12 We sing a song. → ______
우리는 노래를 부른다.

**Words**

□ at night 밤에 □ play the piano 피아노를 연주하다 □ fruit 과일 □ music 음악
□ on the floor 바닥에서 □ library 도서관 □ wash the dishes 설거지를 하다

정답 및 해설 p. 8

## 2 다음 우리말과 일치하도록 괄호 안에서 알맞은 것을 고르세요.

01 We ( read / cook ) dinner at seven.
우리는 7시에 저녁식사를 요리한다.

02 I ( run / wash ) the dishes.
나는 설거지를 한다.

03 We ( go / run ) to school every day.
우리는 매일 학교에 간다.

04 They ( play / like ) soccer after school.
그들은 방과 후에 축구를 한다.

05 We ( walk / run ) to the bus stop.
우리는 버스 정류장에 걸어간다.

06 You ( buy / want ) apples.
너는 사과들을 산다.

07 The horses ( like / cook ) carrots.
그 말들은 당근들을 좋아한다.

08 I ( have / buy ) a computer.
나는 컴퓨터를 가지고 있다.

09 They ( work / stay ) at a hospital.
그들은 병원에서 일한다.

10 I ( drink / eat ) milk in the morning.
나는 아침에 우유를 마신다.

11 We ( work / stay ) at a hotel.
우리는 호텔에 머문다.

12 They ( do / eat ) rice.
그들은 쌀을 먹는다.

**Words**

□ every day 매일 □ after school 방과 후(에) □ bus stop 버스 정류장 □ carrot 당근
□ hospital 병원 □ in the morning 아침에 □ hotel 호텔 □ rice 쌀

## 1 다음 우리말과 일치하도록 보기의 단어를 이용하여 빈칸에 알맞은 말을 쓰세요.

| walk | drink | go | have | study |
|---|---|---|---|---|
| play | watch | work | like | cook |

**01** We ____walk____ to school every day.
우리는 매일 학교에 걸어간다.

**02** The dogs ________________ long tails.
그 개들은 긴 꼬리를 가지고 있다.

**03** We ________________ milk in the morning.
우리는 아침에 우유를 마신다.

**04** They ________________ to the museum every Sunday.
그들은 매주 일요일 박물관에 간다.

**05** I ________________ English in the afternoon.
나는 오후에 영어를 공부한다.

**06** I ________________ dinner.
나는 저녁식사를 요리한다.

**07** We ________________ computer games.
우리는 컴퓨터 게임을 한다.

**08** You ________________ TV.
너는 TV를 본다.

**09** We ________________ spaghetti.
우리는 스파게티를 좋아한다.

**10** They ________________ at a hospital.
그들은 병원에서 일한다.

**Words**

☐ every day 매일 ☐ tail 꼬리 ☐ museum 박물관 ☐ in the afternoon 오후에
☐ computer game 컴퓨터 게임 ☐ spaghetti 스파게티 ☐ hospital 병원

## 2 다음 우리말과 일치하도록 보기의 단어를 이용하여 빈칸에 알맞은 말을 쓰세요.

| eat | drink | run | teach | wash |
|---|---|---|---|---|
| do | have | talk | read | stay |

01 We ____eat____ pizza every day.
우리는 매일 피자를 먹는다.

02 The horses ________ fast.
그 말들은 빨리 달린다.

03 I ________ orange juice in the morning.
나는 아침에 오렌지 주스를 마신다.

04 I ________ books after school.
나는 방과 후 책을 읽는다.

05 They ________ the dishes.
그들은 설거지를 한다.

06 I ________ on the phone.
나는 전화 통화를 한다.

07 They ________ at a hotel.
그들은 호텔에 머문다.

08 They ________ English.
그들은 영어를 가르친다.

09 We ________ lunch at noon.
우리는 정오에 점심식사를 한다.

10 They ________ homework after school.
그들은 방과 후 숙제를 한다.

**Words**

□ pizza 피자 □ fast 빨리 □ phone 전화(기) □ lunch 점심식사 □ at noon 정오에
□ homework 숙제

# 주어가 3인칭 단수일 때 동사의 변화

## 1 3인칭 단수

1 3인칭이란 나(I), 너(you)를 제외한 지칭이며, 단수는 한 사람 또는 동물이나 사물 한 개를 의미합니다.

2 3인칭 단수에는 he 그 / she 그녀 / it 그것 / the girl 그 소녀 / Mike 마이크(사람 이름) / the lion 그 사자 등이 있습니다.

## 2 일반동사의 3인칭 단수형

1 주어가 3인칭 단수일 때 동사에 s나 es 또는 ies를 붙입니다.

| | | |
|---|---|---|
| 대부분의 동사: s를 붙입니다 | run → runs 달리다<br>walk → walks 걷다 | read → reads 읽다<br>eat → eats 먹다 |
| sh, ch, x로 끝나는 동사: es를 붙입니다 | wash → washes 씻다<br>watch → watches 보다<br>fix → fixes 고치다 | |
| y로 끝나는 동사: y를 지우고 ies를 붙입니다 | study → studies 공부하다<br>cry → cries 울다 | |
| 예외적인 경우 | go → goes 가다<br>have → has 가지다, 먹다 | do → does 하다 |

**TIPS** 주어가 3인칭 단수일 때 [모음+y]로 끝나는 현재형 동사에는 s를 붙입니다.
- play → plays
- buy → buys

2 일반 주어와 3인칭 단수 주어일 때 동사 비교

| 일반 주어 동사 | | 3인칭 단수 주어 동사 | |
|---|---|---|---|
| I / You / They / We | like apples.<br>사과를 좋아한다. | He / She / It | likes apples.<br>사과를 좋아한다. |
| | watch TV.<br>TV를 본다. | | watches TV.<br>TV를 본다. |
| | go to school.<br>학교에 간다. | | goes to school.<br>학교에 간다. |
| | study English.<br>영어를 공부한다. | | studies English.<br>영어를 공부한다. |
| | have a computer.<br>컴퓨터를 갖고 있다. | | has a computer.<br>컴퓨터를 갖고 있다. |

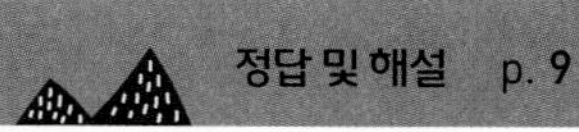
정답 및 해설 p. 9

# 1 다음 규칙에 해당하는 동사를 보기에서 골라 3인칭 단수형을 쓰세요.

| | | | | |
|---|---|---|---|---|
| wash 씻다, 닦다 | study 공부하다 | like 좋아하다 | run 달리다 | eat 먹다 |
| fix 고치다 | read 읽다 | have 가지다, 먹다 | play 놀다 | teach 가르치다 |
| watch 보다 | love 사랑하다 | go 가다 | cry 울다 | do 하다 |

**01** 대부분의 동사: s를 붙입니다.

like → likes　　________ → ________

________ → ________　　________ → ________

________ → ________　　________ → ________

**02** sh, ch, x로 끝나는 동사: es를 붙입니다.

________ → ________　　________ → ________

________ → ________　　________ → ________

**03** [자음+y]로 끝나는 동사: y를 지우고 ies를 붙입니다.

________ → ________　　________ → ________

**04** 예외적인 경우

________ → ________　　________ → ________

________ → ________

**Words**

□ wash 씻다, 닦다　□ like 좋아하다　□ run 달리다　□ read 읽다　□ love 사랑하다
□ watch 보다　□ cry 울다

**1** 다음 괄호 안에서 주어가 3인칭 단수일 때 동사의 형태를 고르고, 단어의 뜻을 쓰세요.

| | | | | |
|---|---|---|---|---|
| 01 | play | (plays) / playes | → | 놀다, 연주하다 |
| 02 | meet | meets / meetes | → | |
| 03 | study | studys / studies | → | |
| 04 | go | go / goes | → | |
| 05 | cook | cooks / cookes | → | |
| 06 | have | haves / has | → | |
| 07 | watch | watchs / watches | → | |
| 08 | cry | cryes / cries | → | |
| 09 | wash | washs / washes | → | |
| 10 | run | runs / runes | → | |
| 11 | buy | buys / buies | → | |
| 12 | drink | drinks / drinkes | → | |

**Words**

☐ play 놀다, 연주하다 ☐ meet 만나다 ☐ go 가다 ☐ cry 울다 ☐ wash 씻다, 닦다
☐ buy 사다 ☐ drink 마시다

정답 및 해설 p. 9

## 2 다음 괄호 안에서 알맞은 것을 고르세요.

01 He ( eat / eats ) dinner at seven.
그는 7시에 저녁을 먹는다.

02 They ( read / reads ) books.
그들은 책을 읽는다.

03 The baby ( crys / cries ) at night.
그 아기는 밤에 운다.

04 Mike ( play / plays ) the piano.
마이크는 피아노를 연주한다.

05 We ( like / likes ) fruit.
우리는 과일들을 좋아한다.

06 She ( love / loves ) music.
그녀는 음악을 사랑한다.

07 We ( sleep / sleeps ) in the bed.
우리는 침대에서 잠을 잔다.

08 The dog ( run / runs ) fast.
그 개는 빨리 달린다.

09 He ( studys / studies ) at the library.
그는 도서관에서 공부한다.

10 She ( have / has ) lunch at noon.
그녀는 정오에 점심식사를 한다.

11 James ( talk / talks ) on the phone.
제임스는 전화 통화를 한다.

12 It ( have / has ) a long tail.
그것은 긴 꼬리를 가지고 있다.

**Words**

- ☐ dinner 저녁식사
- ☐ cry 울다
- ☐ at night 밤에
- ☐ fruit 과일
- ☐ music 음악
- ☐ sleep 잠자다
- ☐ lunch 점심식사
- ☐ at noon 정오에
- ☐ on the phone 전화로

# 1 다음 보기의 단어를 이용하여 문장을 완성하세요. (필요하면 단어를 변형하세요.)

| walk | drink | go | have | study |
|---|---|---|---|---|
| play | watch | work | like | cook |

01 Kevin ___walks___ to school every day.
케빈은 매일 학교에 걸어간다.

02 The dog ________________ a long tail.
그 개는 긴 꼬리를 가지고 있다.

03 My sister ________________ milk in the morning.
나의 누나는 아침에 우유를 마신다.

04 They ________________ to the art gallery every Sunday.
그들은 매주 일요일 미술관에 간다.

05 She ________________ English in the afternoon.
그녀는 오후에 영어를 공부한다.

06 My dad ________________ dinner.
나의 아빠는 저녁식사를 요리한다.

07 I ________________ soccer in the afternoon.
나는 오후에 축구를 한다.

08 We ________________ TV after school.
우리는 방과 후에 TV를 본다.

09 The boy ________________ spaghetti.
그 소년은 스파게티를 좋아한다.

10 The man ________________ at a bank.
그 남자는 은행에서 일한다.

**Words**

□ in the morning 아침에 □ art gallery 미술관 □ every Sunday 매주 일요일(에)
□ in the afternoon 오후에 □ soccer 축구 □ after school 방과 후(에) □ bank 은행

## 2 다음 보기의 단어를 이용하여 문장을 완성하세요. (필요하면 동사를 변형하세요.)

| eat | wash | drink | teach | run |
|---|---|---|---|---|
| do | have | visit | read | stay |

01 She ___eats___ apples every day.
그녀는 매일 사과들을 먹는다.

02 The horse ________ fast.
그 말은 빨리 달린다.

03 We ________ orange juice in the morning.
우리는 아침에 오렌지 주스를 마신다.

04 He ________ books after school.
그는 방과 후 책을 읽는다.

05 Dad ________ the dishes.
아빠는 설거지를 한다.

06 He ________ the museum every day.
그는 매일 박물관을 방문한다.

07 Tom ________ at a hotel.
톰은 호텔에 머문다.

08 Mr. Brian ________ English.
브라이언 씨는 영어를 가르친다.

09 It ________ a long nose.
그것은 긴 코를 가지고 있다.

10 The girl ________ her homework after school.
그 소녀는 방과 후 숙제를 한다.

**Words**

☐ visit 방문하다 ☐ every day 매일 ☐ horse 말 ☐ dish 접시 ☐ museum 박물관
☐ hotel 호텔 ☐ nose 코 ☐ homework 숙제

# Final Check 최종적으로 완성하기

## 1 다음 밑줄 친 부분을 바르게 고쳐 쓰세요.

01 We goes to school every day. → go
우리는 매일 학교에 간다.

02 They eats breakfast at 8 o'clock. → ______
그들은 8시에 아침을 먹는다.

03 The school begin at 9 o'clock. → ______
그 학교는 9시에 시작한다.

04 He have five pencils. → ______
그는 연필 다섯 개를 가지고 있다.

05 She study English at school. → ______
그녀는 학교에서 영어를 공부한다.

06 Jennie watch TV every day. → ______
제니는 매일 TV를 본다.

07 His mom work at a zoo. → ______
그의 엄마는 동물원에서 일한다.

08 I helps poor people. → ______
나는 가난한 사람들을 도와준다.

09 My dog jump high. → ______
나의 개는 높이 뛴다.

10 They has big ears. → ______
그것들은 커다란 귀들을 가지고 있다.

**Words**

□ go to school 학교에 가다 □ breakfast 아침식사 □ o'clock ~시 □ begin 시작하다
□ help 돕다 □ poor 가난한 □ people 사람들 □ jump 뛰다 □ high 높이

## 2 다음 밑줄 친 부분을 바르게 고쳐 쓰세요. (고칠 필요가 없는 곳에는 O표 하세요.)

01 They listens to the radio every day. → listen
그들은 매일 라디오를 듣는다.

02 We play baseball after school. → ______
우리는 방과 후에 야구를 한다.

03 He live in Seoul. → ______
그는 서울에 산다.

04 My friends likes spaghetti. → ______
나의 친구들은 스파게티를 좋아한다.

05 He wash his car on Sundays. → ______
그는 매주 일요일 세차를 한다.

06 Jen do her homework every day. → ______
젠은 매일 숙제를 한다.

07 The store open at 9 o'clock. → ______
그 상점은 9시에 문을 연다.

08 I read books every day. → ______
나는 매일 책을 읽는다.

09 He study English every day. → ______
그는 매일 영어를 공부한다.

10 She love me. → ______
그녀는 나를 사랑한다.

**Words**

□ listen 듣다 □ radio 라디오 □ play baseball 야구를 하다 □ live in ~에 살다
□ spaghetti 스파게티 □ on Sundays 매주 일요일(에) □ store 상점

**1** 다음 중 동사의 뜻이 바르지 않은 것을 고르세요.

① eat – 먹다
② like – 좋아하다
③ walk – 일하다
④ study – 공부하다
⑤ cook – 요리하다

[2-3] 다음 중 동사의 3인칭 단수형이 바르지 않은 것을 고르세요.

**2**
① eat – eats
② love – loves
③ work – works
④ study – studys
⑤ do – does

**3**
① watch – watches
② wash – washs
③ go – goes
④ cook – cooks
⑤ stay – stays

**4** 다음 중 빈칸에 들어갈 알맞은 것을 고르세요.

The boy ______________ dinner at seven.
그 소년은 7시에 저녁식사를 한다.

① have
② has
③ eat
④ haves
⑤ eates

[5-6] 다음 중 밑줄 친 부분이 잘못된 것을 고르세요.

**5**

① She washes her face.

② We likes apples.

③ The baby cries at night.

④ Jake teaches English.

⑤ She has lunch at noon.

5.

3인칭 단수동사에 s나 es를 붙입니다.

**at noon** 정오에

**6**

① She plays computer games.

② We watch TV every day.

③ He works at a hospital.

④ I love James.

⑤ They has five cats.

6.

they는 3인칭 단수가 아닙니다.

**every day** 매일

**7** 다음 주어진 단어를 이용하여 문장을 완성하세요.

(1) She ____________ to school at 9. (go)

그녀는 9시에 학교에 간다.

(2) James ____________ English at the library. (study)

제임스는 도서관에서 영어를 공부한다.

(3) He ____________ milk in the morning. (drink)

그는 아침에 우유를 마신다.

(4) The boy ____________ homework after school. (do)

그 소년은 방과 후 숙제를 한다.

7.

**at 9** 9시에

**library** 도서관

다음 단어의 뜻을 쓰고, 단어를 더 써보세요.

| No. | Word | 뜻 | 쓰기 | No. | Word | 뜻 | 쓰기 |
|---|---|---|---|---|---|---|---|
| 01 | afternoon | 오후 | afternoon | 02 | bank | | |
| 03 | begin | | | 04 | computer | | |
| 05 | cry | | | 06 | floor | | |
| 07 | fruit | | | 08 | gallery | | |
| 09 | homework | | | 10 | hospital | | |
| 11 | hotel | | | 12 | live | | |
| 13 | lunch | | | 14 | meet | | |
| 15 | music | | | 16 | night | | |
| 17 | noon | | | 18 | o'clock | | |
| 19 | people | | | 20 | phone | | |
| 21 | piano | | | 22 | radio | | |
| 23 | sleep | | | 24 | soccer | | |
| 25 | spaghetti | | | 26 | stay | | |
| 27 | study | | | 28 | tail | | |
| 29 | teach | | | 30 | wash | | |

# CHAPTER 6
# 일반동사의 부정문과 의문문

# 일반동사의 부정문

## 일반동사의 부정문 만들기

be동사의 부정문과 달리 일반동사가 있는 문장의 부정문을 만들 때에는 don't나 doesn't를 이용합니다.

1 don't를 사용하는 경우

| | |
|---|---|
| I / You / We / They | don't + 동사원형 ~. |
| 주어가 복수명사(The boys 등) | |

I drink milk. 나는 우유를 마신다.
→ I don't drink milk. 나는 우유를 마시지 않는다.

They drink coffee. 그들은 커피를 마신다.
→ They don't drink coffee. 그들은 커피를 마시지 않는다.

The boys learn English. 그 소년들은 영어를 배운다.
→ The boys don't learn English. 그 소년들은 영어를 배우지 않는다.

2 doesn't을 사용하는 경우 – 주어가 3인칭 단수일 때

| | |
|---|---|
| She / He / It | doesn't + 동사원형 ~. |
| 주어가 단수명사(The girl, Kevin 등) | |

She drinks milk. 그녀는 우유를 마신다.
→ She doesn't drink milk. 그녀는 우유를 마시지 않는다.

He has an apple. 그는 사과를 가지고 있다.
→ He doesn't have an apple. 그는 사과를 가지고 있지 않다. *have의 동사원형은 has입니다.

Kevin learns English. 캐빈은 영어를 배운다.
→ Kevin doesn't learn English. 캐빈은 영어를 배우지 않는다.

TIPS 동사원형이란 동사 원래의 모양을 말하는 것으로 동사에 s나 es를 붙이지 않습니다.
plays, watches 등의 동사원형은 play, watch 등입니다.

# Warm Up

정답 및 해설 p. 10

## 1 다음 괄호 안에서 알맞은 것을 고르세요.

01 I ( don't / doesn't ) have a computer.
나는 컴퓨터가 없다.

02 We ( don't / doesn't ) learn English.
우리는 영어를 배우지 않는다.

03 Tom ( don't / doesn't ) have a bike.
톰은 자전거가 없다.

04 She ( don't / doesn't ) play the guitar.
그녀는 기타를 연주하지 않는다.

05 It ( don't / doesn't ) have a tail.
그것은 꼬리가 없다.

06 My friends ( don't / doesn't ) swim in the river.
내 친구들은 강에서 수영하지 않는다.

07 You ( don't / doesn't ) drink coffee.
너는 커피를 마시지 않는다.

08 My dog ( don't / doesn't ) like balls.
내 개는 공들을 좋아하지 않는다.

09 John ( don't / doesn't ) eat meat.
존은 고기를 먹지 않는다.

10 They ( don't / doesn't ) watch TV.
그들은 TV를 보지 않는다.

### Words

□ computer 컴퓨터 □ learn 배우다 □ bike 자전거 □ play the guitar 기타를 연주하다
□ tail 꼬리 □ swim 수영하다 □ in the river 강에서 □ ball 공 □ meat 고기

## 1 다음 우리말과 일치하도록 빈칸에 알맞은 말을 쓰세요.

01 I ___don't___ like apples.
나는 사과들을 좋아하지 않는다.

02 He ____________ listen to music.
그는 음악을 듣지 않는다.

03 Kevin ____________ eat breakfast.
캐빈은 아침식사를 먹지 않는다.

04 We ____________ go swimming every day.
우리는 매일 수영하러 가지 않는다.

05 He ____________ wash the dishes every day.
그는 매일 설거지를 하지 않는다.

06 They ____________ have rice.
그들은 쌀이 없다.

07 Mary ____________ drink coffee.
메리는 커피를 마시지 않는다.

08 The students ____________ learn English.
그 학생들은 영어를 배우지 않는다.

09 They ____________ work at a bank.
그들은 은행에서 일하지 않는다.

10 She ____________ play the violin.
그녀는 바이올린을 연주하지 않는다.

**Words**

□ listen 듣다 □ music 음악 □ breakfast 아침식사 □ go swimming 수영하러 가다
□ every day 매일 □ rice 쌀 □ coffee 커피 □ play the violin 바이올린을 연주하다

## 2 다음 주어진 단어를 이용하여 문장을 완성하세요.

01 그들은 피자를 좋아하지 않는다. (like)

➡ They ___don't like___ pizza.

02 그녀는 매일 피자를 먹지 않는다. (eat)

➡ She ________________ pizza every day.

03 그 소녀는 일본어로 말하지 않는다. (speak)

➡ The girl ________________ Japanese.

04 그는 방과 후 숙제를 하지 않는다. (do)

➡ He ________________ his homework after school.

05 나는 아침에 샤워하지 않는다. (take)

➡ I ________________ a shower in the morning.

06 캐빈은 매일 박물관을 방문하지 않는다. (visit)

➡ Kevin ________________ the museum every day.

07 그는 매일 수영하러 가지 않는다. (go)

➡ He ________________ swimming every day.

08 그 소녀들은 캐나다에서 살지 않는다. (live)

➡ The girls ________________ in Canada.

09 메리는 학교에 걸어가지 않는다. (walk)

➡ Mary ________________ to school.

10 그 소년은 책을 읽지 않는다. (read)

➡ The boy ________________ books.

**Words**

□ pizza 피자 □ Japanese 일본어 □ after school 방과 후(에) □ shower 샤워
□ visit 방문하다 □ museum 박물관 □ walk 걷다 □ read 읽다

## 1 다음 문장을 부정문으로 바꿔 쓰세요.

01 Tom likes tomatoes. 톰은 토마토를 좋아한다.

➡ Tom doesn't like tomatoes.

02 She wears glasses. 그녀는 안경을 쓴다.

➡ She ______________________.

03 Mary has long hair. 메리는 머리가 길다.

➡ Mary ______________________.

04 I study Chinese. 나는 중국어를 공부한다.

➡ I ______________________.

05 We get up early. 우리는 일찍 일어난다.

➡ We ______________________.

06 Kevin drinks milk every day. 캐빈은 매일 우유를 마신다.

➡ Kevin ______________________.

07 He goes swimming every day. 그는 매일 수영하러 간다.

➡ He ______________________.

08 Jim has an elder brother. 짐은 형이 있다.

➡ Jim ______________________.

09 We walk to school. 우리는 학교에 걸어간다.

➡ We ______________________.

10 The students watch TV every day. 그 학생들은 매일 TV를 본다.

➡ The students ______________________.

**Words**

- ☐ tomato 토마토
- ☐ wear 입다, 쓰다
- ☐ glasses 안경
- ☐ Chinese 중국어
- ☐ get up 일어나다
- ☐ early 일찍
- ☐ elder brother 형
- ☐ walk 걷다

## 2 다음 우리말과 일치하도록 보기의 단어를 이용하여 문장을 완성하세요.

| have | use | play | go | wear |
| --- | --- | --- | --- | --- |
| walk | speak | get up | take | want |

01 The girl ___doesn't have___ a bike.
그 소녀는 자전거가 없다.

02 He ________________ to school.
그는 학교에 걸어가지 않는다.

03 We ________________ English.
우리는 영어로 말하지 않는다.

04 Mary ________________ early.
메리는 일찍 일어나지 않는다.

05 He ________________ a cell phone.
그는 휴대전화를 사용하지 않는다.

06 They ________________ computer games.
그들은 컴퓨터 게임을 하지 않는다.

07 We ________________ a pet.
우리는 애완동물을 원하지 않는다.

08 I ________________ glasses.
나는 안경을 쓰지 않는다.

09 She ________________ to the market every day.
그녀는 매일 시장에 가지 않는다.

10 He ________________ a shower in the morning.
그는 아침에 샤워하지 않는다

**Words**

- ☐ speak 말하다
- ☐ get up 일어나다
- ☐ school 학교
- ☐ early 일찍
- ☐ cell phone 휴대전화(기)
- ☐ pet 애완동물
- ☐ market 시장
- ☐ in the morning 아침에

# 일반동사의 의문문

## 1 일반동사의 의문문 만들기

의문문이란 상대방에게 뭔가를 물어보는 문장을 의미합니다. 일반동사가 있는 문장을 의문문으로 만들 때에는 문장 맨 앞에 Do 또는 Does를 붙이고 문장 끝에 물음표(?)를 붙입니다.

1 Do를 붙이는 경우

| Do | I / you / we / they | + 동사원형 ~ ? |
|---|---|---|
| | 복수명사(my friends 등) | |

They like apples. 그들은 사과들을 좋아한다.
→ **Do** they like apples?
The boys like apples. 그 소년들은 사과들을 좋아한다.
→ **Do** the boys like apples?

2 Does를 붙이는 경우 – 주어가 3인칭 단수일 때

| Does | she / he / it | + 동사원형 ~ ? |
|---|---|---|
| | 단수명사(Mary, the boy 등) | |

He has apples. 그는 사과들이 있다.
→ **Does** he have apples?
Mary has apples. 메리는 사과들이 있다.
→ **Does** Mary have apples? *has의 동사원형은 have입니다.

3 의문문의 대답

- 긍정이면 Yes에 do나 does, 부정이면 No에 don't나 doesn't를 사용합니다.
- Do로 시작하면 대답도 do나 don't를 사용하고, Does로 시작하면 does나 doesn't를 사용합니다.

| | | | |
|---|---|---|---|
| 주어가 단수<br>(한 명 또는 한 개) | **Do** you like apples? | Yes, I **do**. | No, I **don't**. |
| | **Does** he/she like apples? | Yes, he/she **does**.<br>No, he/she **doesn't**. | |
| | **Does** it like apples? | Yes, it **does**. | No, it **doesn't**. |
| 주어가 복수<br>(두 명 또는 두 개 이상) | **Do** they like apples? | Yes, they **do**. | No, they **don't**. |
| | **Do** you like apples? | Yes, we **do**. | No, we **don't**. |

정답 및 해설 p. 10

## 1 다음 괄호 안에서 알맞은 것을 고르세요.

01 ( Do / Does ) you like vegetables? 당신은 야채를 좋아하나요?

02 ( Do / Does ) he have a computer? 그는 컴퓨터가 있나요?

03 ( Do / Does ) she live in Korea? 그녀는 한국에 사나요?

04 ( Do / Does ) the boys study English? 그 소년들은 영어를 공부하나요?

05 ( Do / Does ) the students go to school today? 그 학생들은 오늘 학교에 가나요?

06 ( Do / Does ) Mary keep a diary? 메리는 일기를 쓰나요?

07 ( Do / Does ) the horse run fast? 그 말은 빨리 달리나요?

08 ( Do / Does ) the girl speak Korean? 그 소녀는 한국말을 하나요?

09 ( Do / Does ) Kevin like Korean food? 캐빈은 한국 음식을 좋아하나요?

10 ( Do / Does ) it have a tail? 그것은 꼬리가 있나요?

11 ( Do / Does ) they get up early? 그들은 일찍 일어나나요?

12 ( Do / Does ) the boys study at the library? 그 소년들은 도서관에서 공부하나요?

### Words

- □ vegetable 야채
- □ computer 컴퓨터
- □ keep a diary 일기를 쓰다
- □ speak 말하다
- □ Korean food 한국 음식
- □ tail 꼬리
- □ at the library 도서관에서

## 1 다음 빈칸에 알맞은 말을 쓰세요.

01 ___Does___ she have a cat?
그녀는 고양이가 있나요?

02 ________ it run fast?
그것은 빠르게 달리나요?

03 ________ they speak English?
그들은 영어로 말하나요?

04 ________ the boys go to the beach?
그 소년들은 해변에 가나요?

05 ________ Kevin go to the market every day?
캐빈은 매일 시장에 가나요?

06 ________ the girl use a cell phone?
그 소녀는 휴대전화를 사용하나요?

07 ________ the dog have a long tail?
그 개는 긴 꼬리를 가지고 있나요?

08 ________ your mom like apples?
당신의 어머니는 사과를 좋아하나요?

09 ________ you listen to music every day?
당신은 매일 음악을 듣나요?

10 ________ the baby cry at night?
그 아기는 밤에 우나요?

11 ________ Susan play the piano?
수잔은 피아노를 연주하나요?

12 ________ the students do their homework after school?
그 학생들은 방과 후에 숙제를 하나요?

**Words**

□ beach 해변 □ market 시장 □ use 사용하다 □ cell phone 휴대전화(기)
□ music 음악 □ cry 울다 □ at night 밤에 □ play the piano 피아노를 연주하다

## 2 다음 빈칸에 알맞은 말을 쓰세요.

01 ___Does___ he have a computer?
그는 컴퓨터가 있나요?

02 ________ the animal have a tail?
그 동물은 꼬리가 있나요?

03 ________ they wear school uniforms?
그들은 교복을 입나요?

04 ________ the girls go to the zoo?
그 소녀들은 동물원에 가나요?

05 ________ you go to the library every day?
당신은 매일 도서관에 가나요?

06 ________ Jane have a pet?
제인은 애완동물이 있나요?

07 ________ the dogs run fast?
그 개들은 빨리 달리나요?

08 ________ the students like pizza?
그 학생들은 피자를 좋아하나요?

09 ________ your friends listen to music every day?
당신의 친구들은 매일 음악을 듣나요?

10 ________ the student play the piano?
그 학생은 피아노를 연주하나요?

11 ________ your younger brothers like fruit?
당신의 남동생들은 과일들을 좋아하나요?

12 ________ the woman have a car?
그 여자는 자동차가 있나요?

**Words**

☐ computer 컴퓨터 ☐ animal 동물 ☐ uniform 유니폼 ☐ zoo 동물원 ☐ pet 애완동물
☐ listen to music 음악을 듣다 ☐ younger brother 남동생 ☐ fruit 과일

# 1 다음 빈칸에 알맞은 말을 쓰세요.

01 ___Does___ he like apples? Yes, ___he does___.
그는 사과를 좋아하나요?

02 ________ she drink milk in the morning? Yes, ____________.
그녀는 아침에 우유를 마시나요?

03 ________ the boy wear glasses? Yes, ____________.
그 소년은 안경을 쓰나요?

04 ________ the horses run fast? Yes, ____________.
그 말들은 빨리 달리나요?

05 ________ she go swimming every day? Yes, ____________.
그녀는 매일 수영을 하러 가나요?

06 ________ the girl play basketball after school? No, ____________.
그 소녀는 방과 후에 농구를 하나요?

07 ________ the students wear school uniforms? No, ____________.
그 학생들은 교복을 입나요?

08 ________ your mom have a car? No, ____________.
당신의 어머니는 자동차가 있나요?

09 ________ they play soccer? No, ____________.
그들은 축구를 하나요?

10 ________ the boys listen to the radio? Yes, ____________.
그 소년들은 라디오를 듣나요?

11 ________ the man work at a bank? No, ____________.
그 남자는 은행에서 일하나요?

12 ________ she study English? No, ____________.
그녀는 영어를 공부하나요?

**Words**

- ☐ glasses 안경 ☐ horse 말 ☐ play basketball 농구를 하다 ☐ school uniform 교복
- ☐ soccer 축구 ☐ listen 듣다 ☐ bank 은행

## 2 다음 문장을 의문문으로 바꿔 쓰세요.

01 They like watermelon. 그들은 수박을 좋아한다.

➡ Do they like watermelon?

02 She eats fresh vegetables. 그녀는 신선한 야채들을 먹는다.

➡ ______

03 He reads every day. 그는 매일 책을 읽는다.

➡ ______

04 Tom visits the museum every day. 톰은 매일 박물관을 방문한다.

➡ ______

05 The boy takes a shower in the morning. 그 소년은 아침에 샤워를 한다.

➡ ______

06 The girls have bikes. 그 소녀들은 자전거들이 있다.

➡ ______

07 My mom has a scarf. 나의 엄마는 스카프가 있다.

➡ ______

08 Mina goes shopping. 미나는 쇼핑을 간다.

➡ ______

09 Helen has a computer. 헬렌은 컴퓨터가 있다.

➡ ______

10 The rabbits run fast. 그 토끼들은 빨리 달린다.

➡ ______

**Words**

- ☐ watermelon 수박 ☐ fresh 신선한 ☐ visit 방문하다 ☐ museum 박물관
- ☐ take a shower 샤워하다 ☐ scarf 스카프 ☐ go shopping 쇼핑하러 가다

## 1 다음 밑줄 친 부분을 바르게 고쳐 쓰세요.

01 Do she speak English? → Does
그녀는 영어로 말을 하나요?

02 We doesn't play computer games. → ______
우리는 컴퓨터 게임을 하지 않는다.

03 She doesn't has a computer. → ______
그녀는 컴퓨터가 없다.

04 Does the girls like pizza? → ______
그 소녀들은 피자를 좋아하나요?

05 He doesn't goes to school on weekends. → ______
그는 주말에는 학교에 가지 않는다.

06 Does they swim in the river? → ______
그들은 강에서 수영하나요?

07 Does you have a pet? → ______
당신은 애완동물이 있나요?

08 A: Does the boy have a brother? 그 소년은 형제가 있나요?
B: Yes, he do. → ______

09 A: Does the store open every day? 그 상점은 매일 운영하나요?
B: No, it does. → ______

10 A: Do you drink milk in the morning? 당신(들)은 아침에 우유를 마시나요?
B: Yes, you do. → ______

**Words**

- ☐ computer game 컴퓨터 게임
- ☐ on weekends 주말마다
- ☐ in the river 강에서
- ☐ pet 애완동물
- ☐ store 상점
- ☐ open 열다, 운영하다

## 2 다음 문장을 주어진 지시대로 바꿔 쓰세요.

01 She wears glasses. 그녀는 안경을 쓴다.
➡ 부정문 She doesn't wear glasses.

02 He has a brother. 그는 형제가 있다.
➡ 의문문 ______________________

03 The girl plays the piano. 그 소녀는 피아노를 연주한다.
➡ 부정문 ______________________

04 The girls live in Korea. 그 소녀들은 한국에 산다.
➡ 의문문 ______________________

05 Jennie goes to the shopping mall every day. 제니는 매일 쇼핑몰에 간다.
➡ 의문문 ______________________

06 They help my mom. 그들은 나의 엄마를 돕는다.
➡ 부정문 ______________________

07 Her parents work at a restaurant. 그녀의 부모님들은 식당에서 일한다.
➡ 의문문 ______________________

08 The boy likes pizza. 그 소년은 피자를 좋아한다.
➡ 의문문 ______________________

09 My friends listen to music every day. 내 친구들은 매일 음악을 듣는다.
➡ 부정문 ______________________

10 We walk to school. 우리는 학교에 걸어간다.
➡ 부정문 ______________________

**Words**

☐ live in ~에 살다 ☐ shopping mall 쇼핑몰 ☐ help 돕다 ☐ parent 부모
☐ restaurant 식당 ☐ listen to ~을 듣다 ☐ every day 매일

## Exercise CHAPTER 6

[1-2] 다음 중 빈칸에 들어갈 알맞은 것을 고르세요.

**1**

We ____________ speak English.
우리는 영어로 말하지 않는다.

① don't ② isn't ③ aren't
④ doesn't ⑤ does

**2**

He ____________ like apples.
그는 사과를 좋아하지 않는다.

① don't ② isn't ③ aren't
④ doesn't ⑤ does

[3-4] 다음 중 대화의 빈칸에 들어갈 알맞은 것을 고르세요.

**3**

A: Do they like watermelon?
B: Yes, ______________________.

① I do ② we do ③ he does
④ they do ⑤ you do

**4**

A: Do the boys wear school uniforms?
B: No, ______________________.

① I don't ② we don't ③ he doesn't
④ they don't ⑤ you don't

1.
주어 We는 복수입니다.

2.
He는 3인칭 단수입니다.

3.
인칭대명사로 물으면 인칭대명사로 대답합니다.

4.
주어가 the boys 복수입니다.

## 5 다음 중 밑줄 친 부분이 잘못된 것을 고르세요.

① We don't eat rice.

② He doesn't has a car.

③ Do you go to the museum?

④ Does he drink coffee?

⑤ Do the boys listen to the radio?

5.
doesn't나 don't 다음에는 동사원형이 와야 합니다.

## 6 다음 문장을 부정문으로 바꿔 쓰세요.

(1) He cooks dinner.

➡ ______________________________

(2) The boy goes to school.

➡ ______________________________

(3) The students study English.

➡ ______________________________

## 7 다음 대화의 빈칸에 들어갈 알맞은 대답을 쓰세요.

(1) A: Does he watch TV?

B: Yes, ________________.

(2) A: Does she have a dog?

B: No, ________________.

(3) A: Do they have breakfast?

B: Yes, ________________.

(4) A: Do you like apples?

B: Yes, ________________.

다음 단어의 뜻을 쓰고, 단어를 더 써보세요.

| | | | | | | | |
|---|---|---|---|---|---|---|---|
| 01 | basketball | 농구 | basketball | 02 | beach | | |
| 03 | bike | | | 04 | breakfast | | |
| 05 | coffee | | | 06 | diary | | |
| 07 | drink | | | 08 | early | | |
| 09 | glasses | | | 10 | guitar | | |
| 11 | Japanese | | | 12 | learn | | |
| 13 | listen | | | 14 | market | | |
| 15 | meat | | | 16 | milk | | |
| 17 | pet | | | 18 | rice | | |
| 19 | river | | | 20 | scarf | | |
| 21 | shopping | | | 22 | shower | | |
| 23 | speak | | | 24 | swim | | |
| 25 | uniform | | | 26 | use | | |
| 27 | vegetable | | | 28 | violin | | |
| 29 | visit | | | 30 | wear | | |

# CHAPTER 7
# 인칭대명사 Ⅱ

UNIT 01 my / your / me / you

UNIT 02 He / She / They / It의 쓰임

# my / your / me / you

## 1 소유를 나타내는 표현(소유격) - my, your, his, her

my, your, his, her 등은 명사 앞에 와서 명사의 소유 관계를 나타낼 때 사용합니다.
주로 '~의'라는 의미를 가지고 있으며, 소유격이라고 부릅니다.

my book 나의 책　　your book 너의 책　　his book 그의 책

## 2 목적어 자리에 오는 인칭대명사(목적격) - me, you, him, her

me, you, him, her 등은 목적격이라고 부르며, 문장에서 주어가 아닌 목적어 역할을 합니다. 목적어란 문장에서 '무엇을' 또는 '누구를'에 해당하는 부분입니다. 이러한 목적어는 주로 동사 바로 뒤에 위치합니다.

I love you. 나는 너를 사랑한다.
He loves me. 그는 나를 사랑한다.
We love her. 우리는 그녀를 사랑한다.
I love them. 나는 그들을 사랑한다.

## 3 소유격과 목적격 Ⅰ

| 주격 | 소유격 | 목적격 |
|---|---|---|
| I 나는 | my 나의 | me 나를 |
| you 너는 | your 너의 | you 너를 |
| he 그는 | his 그의 | him 그를 |
| she 그녀는 | her 그녀의 | her 그녀를 |
| it 그것은 | its 그것의 | it 그것을 |

TIPS
- you와 it은 주격과 목적격의 모양이 같습니다.
- 소유격은 혼자서는 사용할 수 없으며 반드시 명사와 함께 와야 합니다.
  예) her dog 그녀의 개　　my cat 나의 고양이

## 4 소유격과 목적격 Ⅱ

| 주격 | 소유격 | 목적격 |
|---|---|---|
| we 우리는 | our 우리의 | us 우리를 |
| they 그들은 / 그것들은 | their 그들의 / 그것들의 | them 그들을 / 그것들을 |
| you 너희들은 | your 너희들의 | you 너희들을 |

# Warm Up

정답 및 해설 p. 12

## 1 다음 표의 빈칸을 채우세요.

| I | my | me |
| --- | --- | --- |
| 나는 | 나의 | 나를 |
| you | your | |
| 너는 | | 너를 |
| he | | |
| 그는 | 그의 | 그를 |
| she | her | |
| 그녀는 | | 그녀를 |
| it | its | |
| 그것은 | | 그것을 |

| we | | |
| --- | --- | --- |
| 우리는 | 우리의 | 우리를 |
| they | their | |
| 그들은 / 그것들은 | | 그들을 / 그것들을 |
| you | | |
| 너희들은 | 너희들의 | 너희들을 |

**Words**

□ my 나의 □ your 너의 □ her 그녀의, 그녀를 □ their 그들의, 그것들의

## 1 다음 우리말과 일치하도록 괄호 안에서 알맞은 것을 고르세요.

01 He is ( my / your ) friend.
그는 나의 친구다.

02 Kevin likes ( their / them ).
캐빈은 그들을 좋아한다.

03 It is ( her / his ) bike.
그것은 그의 자전거다.

04 He drinks ( its / it ) in the morning.
그는 아침에 그것을 마신다.

05 He teaches ( our / us ) every day.
그는 매일 우리를 가르친다.

06 They love ( his / him ).
그들은 그를 사랑한다.

07 He takes care of ( their / our ) cats.
그는 우리의 고양이들을 돌본다.

08 Mary likes ( it / its ).
메리는 그것을 좋아한다.

09 ( Its / It ) tail is short.
그것의 꼬리는 짧다..

10 I visit ( his / him ) every day.
나는 매일 그를 방문한다.

**Words**

☐ friend 친구 ☐ bike 자전거 ☐ in the morning 아침에 ☐ every day 매일
☐ take care of ~을 돌보다 ☐ tail 꼬리

정답 및 해설 p. 12

## 2 다음 우리말과 일치하도록 괄호 안에서 알맞은 것을 고르세요.

01 Jim is ( she / her ) friend.

짐은 그녀의 친구다.

02 Jake helps ( our / us ).

제이크는 우리를 도와준다.

03 It is ( my / me ) camera.

그것은 나의 카메라다.

04 They are ( his / him ) candies.

그것들은 그의 사탕들이다.

05 ( She / Her ) hair is long.

그녀의 머리카락은 길다.

06 I like ( her / his ) songs.

나는 그의 노래들을 좋아한다.

07 They aren't ( me / my ) dogs. They are ( her / his ) dogs.

그것들은 나의 개들이 아니다. 그것들은 그녀의 개들이다.

08 It isn't ( my / me ) ball. It is ( his / him ) ball.

그것은 나의 공이 아니다. 그것은 그의 공이다.

09 They aren't ( your / you ) parents. They are ( our / us ) parents.

그들은 너의 부모님들이 아니다. 그들은 우리의 부모님들이다.

10 They aren't ( my / me ) pencils. They are ( their / them ) pencils.

그것들은 나의 연필들이 아니다. 그것들은 그들의 연필들이다.

**Words**

□ help 돕다 □ camera 카메라 □ candy 사탕 □ hair 머리카락 □ song 노래
□ ball 공 □ parent 부모 □ pencil 연필

## 1 다음 우리말과 일치하도록 빈칸에 알맞은 말을 쓰세요.

**01** Dad washes ___his___ face.
아빠가 그의 얼굴을 닦는다.

**02** ________ teacher is very kind.
우리의 선생님은 매우 친절하다.

**03** It isn't ________ school.
그것은 그들의 학교가 아니다.

**04** She brushes ________ teeth in the morning.
그녀는 아침에 그녀의 이를 닦는다.

**05** My parents love ________.
나의 부모님은 나를 사랑한다.

**06** They like ________ hair style.
그들은 그의 머리 모양을 좋아한다.

**07** ________ mom works at a bookstore.
그의 엄마는 서점에서 일한다.

**08** John wants ________.
존은 그것들을 원한다.

**09** We visit ________ store every day.
우리는 매일 그의 가게를 방문한다.

**10** It is ________ room.
그것은 우리의 방이다.

**Words**

□ wash one's face 세수하다 □ kind 친절한 □ brush one's teeth 양치하다 □ style 모양
□ bookstore 서점 □ store 가게

정답 및 해설 p. 12

## 2 다음 우리말과 일치하도록 빈칸에 알맞은 말을 쓰세요.

01 She is ___their___ grandmother.
그녀는 그들의 할머니다.

02 __________ elder brother is very tall.
그의 형은 매우 키가 크다.

03 I like __________ color.
나는 그것의 색깔을 좋아한다.

04 She invites __________ to the party.
그녀는 나를 파티에 초대한다.

05 James buys __________ at a convenience store.
제임스는 그것을 편의점에서 산다.

06 They aren't __________ bags. They are __________ bags.
그것들은 우리의 가방들이 아니다. 그것들은 그의 가방들이다.

07 It isn't __________ cat. It is __________ cat.
그것은 나의 고양이가 아니다. 그것은 그녀의 고양이다.

08 They aren't __________ books. They are __________ books.
그것들은 너의 책들이 아니다. 그것들은 그들의 책들이다.

09 They aren't __________ socks. They are __________ socks.
그것들은 우리의 양말들이 아니다. 그것들은 그들의 양말들이다.

10 He doesn't meet __________. He meets __________.
그는 그녀를 만나지 않는다. 그는 그들을 만난다.

**Words**

- ☐ grandmother 할머니
- ☐ tall 키가 큰
- ☐ color 색깔
- ☐ invite 초대하다
- ☐ party 파티
- ☐ convenience store 편의점
- ☐ sock 양말
- ☐ meet 만나다

# He / She / They / It의 쓰임

## 1 He / She / They / It의 쓰임

| | |
|---|---|
| He는 '그는'이란 의미로 앞에서 언급한 남성 한 명을 대신해 사용합니다. | There is a boy in the classroom. 한 소년이 교실에 있다.<br>He is tall. (He = The boy) 그는 키가 크다. |
| She는 '그녀는'이란 의미로 앞에서 언급한 여성 한 명을 대신해 사용합니다. | There is a girl in the classroom. 한 소녀가 교실에 있다.<br>She is tall. (She = The girl) 그녀는 키가 크다. |
| They는 '그(것)들은'이란 의미로 앞에서 언급한 둘 이상의 사람, 사물, 동물들을 대신해 사용합니다. | There are three boys in the classroom.<br>세 명의 소년들이 교실에 있다.<br>They are tall. (Three boys = They) 그들은 키가 크다.<br>The apples are in the basket. 그 사과들은 바구니에 있다.<br>They are fresh. (They = The apples) 그것들은 신선한다. |
| It은 '그것은'이란 의미로 앞에서 언급한 한 개의 물건이나 동물 한 마리를 대신해 사용합니다. | The computer is on the desk. 그 컴퓨터는 책상 위에 있다.<br>It is broken. ( It = The computer) 그것은 고장 났다. |

## 2 him / her / them / us / it의 쓰임

| | |
|---|---|
| him은 '그를'이란 의미로 앞에서 언급한 남성 한 명을 대신해 사용합니다. | Kevin is my friend. 캐빈은 나의 친구다.<br>I like him. (him = Kevin) 나는 그를 좋아한다. |
| her는 '그녀를'이란 의미로 앞에서 언급한 여성 한 명을 대신해 사용합니다. | Jane is my friend. 제인은 나의 친구다.<br>I like her. (her = Jane) 나는 그녀를 좋아한다. |
| them은 '그(것)들을'이란 의미로 앞에서 언급한 둘 이상의 사람, 사물, 동물들을 대신해 사용합니다. | John and Tom are my friends. 존과 톰은 나의 친구들이다.<br>I like them. (them = John and Tom) 나는 그들을 좋아한다. |
| us는 '우리를'이란 의미로 나를 포함한 두 명 이상의 사람을 대신해 사용합니다. | Bob and I are students. 밥과 나는 학생들이다.<br>Jim teaches us. (us = Bob and I) 짐은 우리를 가르친다. |
| it은 '그것을'이란 의미로 앞에서 언급한 사물이나 동물 하나를 대신해 사용합니다. | The computer is very old. 그 컴퓨터는 매우 오래됐다.<br>I don't want it. (it = the computer) 나는 그것을 원하지 않는다. |

# Warm Up

정답 및 해설 p. 12

## 1 다음 괄호 안에서 알맞은 것을 고르세요.

01 There are three boys in the room. ( He / She / They ) are my friends.
세 명의 소년들이 방에 있다. 그들은 나의 친구들이다.

02 There is a girl in the classroom. ( He / She / They ) is very tall.
한 소녀가 교실에 있다. 그녀는 매우 키가 크다.

03 My sister is five years old. ( It / She / They ) doesn't go to school.
내 여동생은 5살이다. 그녀는 학교에 가지 않는다.

04 John and Tom are my cousins. I like ( she / him / them ).
존과 톰은 나의 사촌들이다. 나는 그들을 좋아한다.

05 My father is very strict. ( He / She / They ) works at a bank.
나의 아버지는 매우 엄격하다. 그는 은행에서 일한다.

06 The students live in Canada. ( He / She / They ) speak English.
그 학생들은 캐나다에 산다. 그들은 영어로 말한다.

07 Jane is my sister. I love ( her / him / them ).
제인은 나의 여동생이다. 나는 그녀를 사랑한다.

08 My dog is very cute. I love ( it / its / them ).
나의 개는 매우 귀엽다. 나는 그것을 사랑한다.

09 Bob and I learn English. Jessy teaches ( her / him / us ).
밥과 나는 영어를 배운다. 제시는 우리를 가르친다.

10 My uncle is a farmer. I visit ( she / him / them ) every weekend.
나의 삼촌은 농부다. 나는 주말마다 그를 방문한다.

### Words

□ in the classroom 교실에 □ go to school 학교에 가다 □ cousin 사촌 □ strict 엄격한
□ English 영어 □ cute 귀여운 □ learn 배우다 □ farmer 농부 □ visit 방문하다

## 1 다음 우리말과 일치하도록 빈칸에 알맞은 말을 쓰세요.

**01** My mom works at a restaurant. ___She___ is a cook.
나의 엄마는 식당에서 일한다. 그녀는 요리사다.

**02** The boy is on the stage. ________ is a singer.
그 소년이 무대 위에 있다. 그는 가수다.

**03** My cousin is fourteen years old. ________ goes to middle school.
나의 사촌은 14살이다. 그는 중학교에 다닌다.

**04** John and Jane are my friends. I like ________.
존과 제인은 내 친구들이다. 나는 그들을 좋아한다.

**05** My girlfriend is very tall. ________ is a basketball player.
나의 여자 친구는 매우 키가 크다. 그녀는 농구 선수다.

**06** The boys live in China. ________ speak Chinese.
그 소년들은 중국에 산다. 그들은 중국어로 말한다.

**07** Tom is my elder brother. I love ________.
톰은 나의 형이다. 나는 그를 사랑한다.

**08** My uncle is a policeman. ________ wears a uniform.
나의 삼촌은 경찰이다. 그는 제복을 입는다.

**09** My mom is a nurse. I love ________.
나의 엄마는 간호사다. 나는 그녀를 사랑한다.

**10** The strawberries are in the basket. ________ are very fresh.
그 딸기들이 바구니에 있다. 그것들은 매우 신선하다.

**Words**

- ☐ restaurant 식당
- ☐ stage 무대
- ☐ middle school 중학교
- ☐ player 선수
- ☐ Chinese 중국어
- ☐ policeman 경찰
- ☐ uniform 제복
- ☐ fresh 신선한

정답 및 해설 p. 12

## 2 다음 우리말과 일치하도록 빈칸에 알맞은 말을 쓰세요.

01 My friends are baseball players. They play baseball on Sunday.
나의 친구들은 야구 선수들이다. 그들은 일요일에 야구를 한다.

02 Two women are on stage. ________ are pianists.
두 명의 여자들이 무대 위에 있다. 그들은 피아니스트들이다.

03 My backpack is red. ________ is on the desk.
나의 배낭은 빨간색이다. 그것은 책상 위에 있다.

04 Mina and Jinsu are Korean. ________ live in Busan.
미나와 진수는 한국인들이다. 그들은 부산에 산다.

05 The apples are in the basket. ________ are fresh.
그 사과들이 바구니에 있다. 그것들은 신선하다.

06 The cat is on the sofa. ________ has a long tail.
그 고양이가 소파 위에 있다. 그것은 긴 꼬리를 가지고 있다.

07 The car is in the garage. ________ is red.
그 자동차는 차고에 있다. 그것은 빨간색이다.

08 We learn Chinese. Mr. Jang teaches ________.
우리는 중국어를 배운다. 장 선생님이 우리를 가르친다.

09 The computer is broken. I don't use ________.
그 컴퓨터는 고장 났다. 나는 그것을 사용하지 않는다.

10 They are my grandparents. I love ________ very much.
그들은 나의 조부모님들이다. 나는 그들을 매우 많이 사랑한다.

**Words**

☐ baseball player 야구 선수 ☐ pianist 피아니스트 ☐ backpack 배낭
☐ on the sofa 소파 위에 ☐ garage 차고 ☐ broken 고장 난 ☐ grandparent 조부모

## 1 다음 우리말과 일치하도록 밑줄 친 부분을 바르게 고쳐 쓰세요.

**01** My dad works at a hospital. She is a doctor. → He
나의 아빠는 병원에서 일한다. 그는 의사다.

**02** Five girls are on stage. She are singers. → ______
다섯 명의 소녀들이 무대 위에 있다. 그들은 가수들이다.

**03** The book is interesting. I read them every day. → ______
그 책은 재미있다. 나는 그것을 매일 읽는다.

**04** John and Jane are my friends. We are diligent. → ______
존과 제인은 내 친구들이다. 그들은 부지런하다.

**05** Tom and I are students. I go to school every day. → ______
톰과 나는 학생이다. 우리는 매일 학교에 간다.

**06** The boys are Korean. We live in Busan. → ______
그 소년들은 한국사람들이다. 그들은 부산에 산다.

**07** Kelly is my younger sister. I love him. → ______
켈리는 나의 여동생이다. 나는 그녀를 사랑한다.

**08** My aunt is very tall. He is a basketball player. → ______
나의 숙모는 매우 키가 크다. 그녀는 농구 선수다.

**09** I have two cats. It like balls. → ______
나는 고양이 두 마리가 있다. 그것들은 공들을 좋아한다.

**10** The boy is in the classroom. She is my friend. → ______
그 소년이 교실에 있다. 그는 내 친구다.

**Words**

□ hospital 병원 □ stage 무대 □ singer 가수 □ interesting 재미있는
□ diligent 부지런한 □ basketball player 농구 선수 □ classroom 교실

정답 및 해설 p. 12

## 2 다음 우리말과 일치하도록 밑줄 친 부분을 바르게 고쳐 쓰세요.

01 His mom works at a hospital. He is a doctor. → She
그의 엄마는 병원에서 일한다. 그녀는 의사다.

02 The show is funny. We watch them every day. → ______
그 쇼는 재미있다. 우리는 그것을 매일 시청한다.

03 We learn English. Mr. Ted teaches me. → ______
우리는 영어를 배운다. 테드 선생님이 우리를 가르친다.

04 The songs are popular. I listen to it every day. → ______
그 노래들은 인기가 있다. 나는 그것들을 매일 듣는다.

05 Ted and Tom come from the U.S. We are teachers. → ______
테드와 톰은 미국에서 왔다. 그들은 선생님들이다.

06 Minsu and I speak Korean. They are Korean. → ______
민수와 나는 한국어로 말한다. 우리는 한국사람들이다.

07 Ms. Kelly is our English teacher. He is very kind. → ______
켈리 씨는 우리의 영어 선생님이다. 그녀는 매우 친절하다.

08 Mr. Johnson is a businessman. She is very busy. → ______
존슨 씨는 사업가다. 그는 매우 바쁘다.

09 I have three dogs. I walk her in the afternoon. → ______
나는 개가 세 마리 있다. 나는 그것들을 오후에 산책시킨다.

10 The pencil is on the table. He is not my pencil. → ______
그 연필이 식탁 위에 있다. 그것은 내 연필이 아니다.

### Words

□ show 쇼 □ funny 재미있는 □ Mr. (남자의 성(명) · 관직명 앞에 붙여) ~씨 □ song 노래
□ popular 인기 있는 □ Ms. (미혼 · 기혼 모든 여성 앞에) ~씨 □ businessman 사업가

## 1 다음 우리말과 일치하도록 밑줄 친 부분을 바르게 고쳐 쓰세요.

01 My sister walks his dog in the morning. ➡ her
내 언니는 아침에 그녀의 개를 산책시킨다.

02 Our teacher is very kind. ➡ ______
나의 선생님은 매우 친절하다.

03 It isn't their dog. ➡ ______
그것은 그의 개가 아니다.

04 He brushes her teeth in the morning. ➡ ______
그는 아침에 그의 이를 닦는다.

05 Our parents love our. ➡ ______
우리 부모님들은 우리를 사랑한다.

06 They love them parents. ➡ ______
그들은 그들의 부모님들을 사랑한다.

07 His mom works at a museum. ➡ ______
그녀의 엄마는 박물관에서 일한다.

08 John wants them. ➡ ______
존은 그것을 원한다.

09 It is us computer. ➡ ______
그것은 우리의 컴퓨터다.

10 They aren't you toys. They are his toys. ➡ ______ ______
그것들은 너의 장난감들이 아니다. 그것들은 그녀의 장난감들이다.

**Words**

☐ walk 산책시키다 ☐ kind 친절 ☐ brush one's teeth 이를 닦다 ☐ parent 부모
☐ museum 박물관 ☐ toy 장난감

## 2 다음 우리말과 일치하도록 빈칸에 보기에서 알맞은 말을 골라 쓰세요.

It　She　He　We　They　them　us　it

01 My brother is tall. ___He___ is a basketball player.
나의 형은 키가 크다. 그는 농구 선수다.

02 Two men are on stage. __________ are actors.
두 명의 남자들이 무대에 있다. 그들은 배우들이다.

03 My car is red. __________ is in the parking lot.
나의 자동차는 빨간색이다. 그것은 주차장에 있다.

04 Mike and I are American. __________ live in Chicago.
마이크와 나는 미국인들이다. 우리는 시카고에 산다.

05 The boys are students. __________ are very smart.
그 소년들은 학생들이다. 그들은 매우 영리하다.

06 My mom is a nurse. __________ works at a hospital.
나의 엄마는 간호사다. 그녀는 병원에서 일한다.

07 Jessie and Tom are my cousins. I love __________.
제시와 톰은 나의 사촌들이다. 나는 그들을 사랑한다.

08 Jisu and I learn English. Mr. Wilson teaches __________.
지수와 나는 영어를 배운다. 윌슨 선생님은 우리를 가르친다.

09 They are my parents. I love __________ very much.
그들은 나의 부모님들이다. 나는 그들을 아주 많이 사랑한다.

10 It is my book. I read __________ every day.
그것은 나의 책이다. 나는 매일 그것을 읽는다.

**Words**

□ on the stage 무대에서　□ actor 배우　□ parking lot 주차장　□ American 미국인
□ nurse 간호사　□ hospital 병원　□ cousin 사촌　□ learn 배우다　□ read 읽다

**1** 다음 중 소유격의 연결이 잘못된 것을 고르세요.

① you – your ② it – its
③ they – them ④ he – his
⑤ she – her

**2** 다음 중 목적격의 연결이 잘못된 것을 고르세요.

① I – me ② it – it
③ she – her ④ he – him
⑤ we – our

**3** 다음 중 빈칸에 올 수 없는 것을 고르세요.

They are ________ dogs.

① my ② her ③ his
④ them ⑤ our

**4** 다음 중 빈칸에 들어갈 알맞은 것을 고르세요.

The book is interesting. I read ________ every day.

① me ② her ③ him
④ them ⑤ it

3.
소유격과 목적격의 쓰임을 알아 보세요.

4.
빈칸에는 the book을 대신하는 목적어가 와야 합니다

정답 및 해설 p. 13

**5** 다음 중 밑줄 친 부분이 잘못된 것을 고르세요.

① I love them.
② It isn't her bag.
③ He loves his parents.
④ Tom visits their every day.
⑤ She has my cookies.

5.
소유격 다음에는 명사가 옵니다. 소유격은 혼자서 동사 다음에 올 수 없습니다.

**6** 다음 중 우리말과 일치하도록 빈칸에 들어갈 말이 바르게 짝지어진 것을 고르세요.

They aren't _____ books. They are _____ books.
그것들은 너희들의 책들이 아니다. 그것들은 그들의 책들이다.

① you – your
② your – their
③ its – your
④ his – their
⑤ their – them

**7** 다음 우리말과 일치하도록 빈칸에 알맞은 말을 쓰세요.

(1) ____________ teacher is very kind.
나의 선생님은 매우 친절하다.

(2) I love ____________ very much.
나는 그녀를 아주 많이 사랑한다.

(3) She visits ____________ every Sunday.
그녀는 매주 일요일 우리를 방문한다.

(4) Jane and Tom are my friends. I love ____________.
제인과 톰은 내 친구들이다. 나는 그들을 사랑한다.

7.
**kind** 친절한
**every Sunday** 매주 일요일

다음 단어의 뜻을 쓰고, 단어를 더 써보세요.

01 backpack 배낭 backpack

02 ball

03 basket

04 bookstore

05 broken

06 businessman

07 candy

08 Chinese

09 color

10 cute

11 face

12 farmer

13 garage

14 grandparent

15 help

16 interesting

17 morning

18 Mr.

19 Ms.

20 parent

21 pianist

22 player

23 policeman

24 popular

25 show

26 song

27 stage

28 store

29 style

30 toy

# CHAPTER 8
# can / be going to

# can의 쓰임

## 1 can의 의미와 형태

| | |
|---|---|
| **긍정문**<br>(can+동사원형) | 의미: can은 '~할 수 있다'라는 의미로 능력을 나타낼 때 사용합니다.<br>형태: can 다음에 반드시 동사원형이 와야 합니다. [주어+can+동사원형~.]<br>I can speak English. 나는 영어로 말할 수 있다.<br>We can run fast. 우리는 빨리 달릴 수 있다. |
| **부정문**<br>(can't+동사원형) | 의미: '~할 수 없다'라는 의미를 나타낼 때 사용합니다.<br>형태: can 뒤에 not을 붙여 cannot의 형태로 쓰고, can't로 줄여 쓸 수 있습니다. [주어+can't[cannot]+동사원형~.]<br>I can't speak English. 나는 영어로 말할 수 없다.<br>We can't run fast. 우리는 빨리 달릴 수 없다. |

TIPS can이나 can't는 주어의 수나 인칭에 상관없이 같은 형태로 사용합니다.

| | |
|---|---|
| I / He / She / They / We / It | **can run** fast.<br>**can't run** fast. |

## 2 can을 이용한 의문문

| | |
|---|---|
| **의문문**<br>(Can+주어+동사원형~?) | 의미: '~할 수 있나요?'라는 의미로 질문할 때 사용합니다.<br>형태: can을 주어 앞으로 보내고 문장 끝에 물음표를 붙입니다. [Can+주어+동사원형~?]<br>Can you speak English? 당신은 영어로 말할 수 있나요?<br>Can they run fast? 그들은 빨리 달릴 수 있나요? |

## 3 대답하기

| 질문 | 긍정의 대답<br>(예, 할 수 있어요.) | 부정의 대답<br>(아니요, 할 수 없어요.) |
|---|---|---|
| **Can** you speak English?<br>**Can** your sister speak English? | Yes, I **can**.<br>Yes, she **can**. | No, I **can't**.<br>No, she **can't**. |

TIPS 질문의 주어가 명사(your sister)라도 대답은 대명사(she)로 합니다.

# Warm Up

정답 및 해설 p. 13

## 1 다음 우리말과 일치하도록 괄호 안에서 알맞은 것을 고르세요.

01 I ( can / can't ) play the violin.
나는 바이올린을 연주할 수 있다.

02 He ( can / can't ) drive a truck.
그는 트럭을 운전할 수 있다.

03 She can ( make / makes ) a cake.
그녀는 케이크를 만들 수 있다.

04 I ( can / can't ) swim in the sea.
나는 바다에서 수영할 수 없다.

05 She ( can / can't ) read a book.
그녀는 책을 읽을 수 있다.

06 We can ( run / runs ) fast.
우리는 빨리 달릴 수 있다.

07 Jane ( can / can't ) ride a bike.
제인은 자전거를 탈 수 없다.

08 My dad ( can / can't ) climb the tree.
나의 아빠는 그 나무에 올라갈 수 있다.

09 ( Can / Do ) you get up early in the morning?
당신은 아침에 일찍 일어날 수 있나요?

10 Tom ( can / can't ) jump high.
톰은 높이 점프할 수 있다.

### Words

□ violin 바이올린 □ drive 운전하다 □ truck 트럭 □ in the sea 바다에서
□ fast 빨리 □ ride a bike 자전거를 타다 □ climb 오르다 □ early 일찍 □ high 높이

## 1 다음 그림을 보고 can이나 can't를 써서 문장을 완성하세요.

01 She ___can___ run fast.
그녀는 빨리 달릴 수 있다.

02 The boy __________ swim.
그 소년은 수영할 수 없다.

03 The girl __________ play the harp.
그 소녀는 하프를 연주할 수 있다.

04 The bird __________ fly high.
그 새는 높이 날 수 있다.

05 The baby __________ walk.
그 아기는 걸을 수 없다.

06 We __________ play basketball.
우리는 농구를 할 수 있다.

07 I __________ wash the dishes.
나는 설거지를 할 수 있다.

08 Josh __________ drive a car.
조쉬는 자동차를 운전할 수 있다.

**Words**

□ swim 수영하다 □ play the harp 하프를 타다 □ play basketball 농구하다
□ wash the dishes 설거지하다 □ drive a car 자동차를 운전하다

정답 및 해설 p. 13

## 2 다음 우리말과 일치하도록 주어진 단어를 이용하여 빈칸에 알맞은 표현을 쓰세요.

01 우리는 중국어로 말할 수 있다. (speak)

→ We ___can___ ___speak___ Chinese.

02 그녀는 그 문제를 풀 수 있다. (solve)

→ She ________ ________ the problem.

03 나는 커피를 마실 수 없다. (drink)

→ I ________ ________ coffee.

04 그는 전화를 받을 수 없다. (answer)

→ He ________ ________ the phone.

05 나는 그것을 읽을 수 없다. (read)

→ I ________ ________ it.

06 그는 바다에서 수영할 수 없다. (swim)

→ He ________ ________ in the sea.

07 우리는 프랑스어를 이해할 수 없다. (understand)

→ We ________ ________ French.

08 그 강아지는 빠르게 달릴 수 없다. (run)

→ The puppy ________ ________ fast.

09 그들은 그 집에 들어갈 수 있다. (enter)

→ They ________ ________ the house.

10 나의 아빠는 말을 탈수 있다. (ride)

→ My dad ________ ________ a horse.

**Words**

□ Chinese 중국어 □ solve 풀다 □ answer 대답하다 □ phone 전화(기)
□ understand 이해하다 □ French 프랑스어 □ enter 들어가다 □ ride 타다

# 1 다음 우리말과 일치하도록 주어진 단어를 이용하여 빈칸에 알맞은 표현을 쓰세요.

**01** A: 당신의 아버지는 말을 탈 수 있나요?
B: 예, 탈 수 있어요.
A: ___Can___ your dad ___ride___ a horse? (ride)
B: Yes, ___he___ ___can___.

**02** A: 당신은 설거지를 할 수 있나요?
B: 예, 할 수 있어요.
A: __________ you __________ the dishes? (wash)
B: Yes, __________ __________.

**03** A: 당신의 엄마는 기타를 칠 수 있나요?
B: 아니요, 할 수 없어요.
A: __________ your mom __________ the guitar? (play)
B: No, __________ __________.

**04** A: 당신의 친구들은 중국어를 할 수 있나요?
B: 아니요, 할 수 없어요.
A: __________ your friends __________ Chinese? (speak)
B: No, __________ __________.

**05** A: 당신의 개는 빨리 달릴 수 있나요?
B: 예, 할 수 있어요.
A: __________ your dog __________ fast? (run)
B: Yes, __________ __________.

**Words**
□ horse 말 □ ride 타다 □ dish 접시 □ guitar 기타 □ friend 친구
□ Chinese 중국어 □ fast 빨리

## 2 다음 우리말과 일치하도록 주어진 단어를 이용해서 긍정문과 부정문을 완성하세요.

**01** 나는 피아노를 칠 수 있다. (play)

➡ I ___can___ ___play___ the piano.

➡ 부정문 I ___can't___ ___play___ the piano.

**02** 그녀는 그 질문에 대답할 수 있다. (answer)

➡ She ________ ________ the question.

➡ 부정문 She ________ ________ the question.

**03** 그는 그 자전거를 고칠 수 있다. (fix)

➡ He ________ ________ the bike.

➡ 부정문 He ________ ________ the bike.

**04** 나의 여동생은 노래를 잘할 수 있다. (sing)

➡ My sister ________ ________ well.

➡ 부정문 My sister ________ ________ well.

**05** 그 소년들은 그 경기를 이길 수 있다. (win)

➡ The boys ________ ________ the game.

➡ 부정문 The boys ________ ________ the game.

**06** 그의 친구들은 그 파티에 올 수 있다. (come)

➡ His friends ________ ________ to the party.

➡ 부정문 His friends ________ ________ to the party.

**07** 나의 삼촌은 피자를 만들 수 있다. (make)

➡ My uncle ________ ________ pizza.

➡ 부정문 My uncle ________ ________ pizza.

**Words**

☐ play 연주하다 ☐ piano 피아노 ☐ answer 대답하다 ☐ question 질문 ☐ fix 고치다
☐ win 이기다 ☐ game 경기 ☐ party 파티

# be going to의 쓰임

## 1 be going to의 의미와 형태

| | |
|---|---|
| **긍정문**<br>(be동사+going to<br>+동사원형) | 의미: '~할 것이다'라는 의미로 앞으로 일어날 일을 계획하거나, 예측할 때 사용합니다.<br>형태: be going to 다음에 반드시 동사원형이 와야 합니다.<br>[주어+be going to+동사원형~.]<br>I am going to visit her tomorrow. 나는 내일 그녀를 방문할 것이다.<br>She is going to be ten next year. 그녀는 내년에 10살이 될 것이다. |
| **부정문**<br>(be동사+not+going<br>to+동사원형) | 의미: '~하지 않을 것이다'라는 의미를 나타낼 때 사용합니다.<br>형태: be동사 다음에 not을 넣습니다.<br>[주어+be동사+not+going to+동사원형~.]<br>I am not going to visit her tomorrow. 나는 내일 그녀를 방문하지 않을 것이다. |

TIPS
- be going to를 사용할 때 be동사는 주어의 수나 인칭에 따라 다르게 사용해야 합니다.

| | |
|---|---|
| I | am[am not] going to visit her tomorrow. |
| He / She / It | is[is not] going to visit her tomorrow. |
| You / They / We | are[are not] going to visit her tomorrow. |

- be going to 대신 will(~할 것이다)을 사용할 수도 있습니다.
  I am going to visit her tomorrow. → I will visit her tomorrow.

## 2 be going to를 이용한 의문문

| | |
|---|---|
| **의문문**<br>(Be동사+주어+going to<br>+동사원형?) | 의미: '~할 건가요?'라는 뜻으로 앞으로 일어날 일을 물을 때 사용합니다.<br>형태: be동사를 주어 앞으로 보내고 문장 끝에 물음표를 붙입니다.<br>[Be동사+주어+going to+동사원형~?]<br>Are you going to stay home tomorrow? 당신은 내일 집에 머물 건가요?<br>Is she going to go shopping? 그녀는 쇼핑을 갈 건가요? |

## 3 대답하기

| 질문 | 긍정의 대답<br>(예, 할 거예요.) | 부정의 대답<br>(아니요, 하지 않을 거예요.) |
|---|---|---|
| Are you going to read a book? | Yes, I am. | No, I am not. |
| Is your brother going to stay home tomorrow? | Yes, he is. | No, he isn't. |

TIPS 질문의 주어가 명사(your brother)라도 대답은 대명사(he)로 합니다.

# Warm Up

정답 및 해설 p. 13

## 1 다음 괄호 안에서 알맞은 것을 고르세요.

**01** I ( am going to / am going ) get up early tomorrow.
나는 내일 일찍 일어날 것이다.

**02** I am going to ( play / plays ) tennis after school.
나는 방과 후 테니스를 칠 것이다.

**03** They ( is / are ) going to go fishing tomorrow.
그들은 내일 낚시를 갈 것이다.

**04** She ( is / are ) going to be thirteen next year.
그녀는 내년에 13살이 될 것이다.

**05** My friends ( not are / are not ) going to visit the museum.
내 친구들은 박물관을 방문하지 않을 것이다.

**06** Sam ( not is / is not ) going to eat dinner.
샘은 저녁식사를 먹지 않을 것이다.

**07** The soccer game ( is going to / is going ) start soon.
그 축구 경기가 곧 시작할 것이다.

**08** We are going to ( watch / watches ) a movie tomorrow.
우리는 내일 영화를 볼 것이다.

**09** He is not ( going to / to going ) buy a car.
그는 자동차를 사지 않을 것이다.

**10** Are they ( going to / are going to ) swim in the river?
그들은 강에서 수영할 건가요?

### Words

- ☐ get up 일어나다
- ☐ play tennis 테니스를 치다
- ☐ go fishing 낚시를 가다
- ☐ visit 방문하다
- ☐ start 시작하다
- ☐ soon 곧
- ☐ movie 영화
- ☐ river 강

## 1 다음 우리말과 일치하도록 주어진 단어를 이용하여 문장을 완성하세요.

01 He ___is going to meet___ his friends. (meet)
그는 그의 친구들을 만날 것이다.

02 I ________________ Japan. (visit)
나는 일본을 방문하지 않을 것이다.

03 He ________________ a cell phone. (buy)
그는 휴대전화기를 사지 않을 것이다.

04 They ________________ dinner at the restaurant. (have)
그들은 식당에서 저녁식사를 할 것이다.

05 She ________________ shopping this weekend. (go)
그녀는 이번 주말에 쇼핑을 가지 않을 것이다.

06 Mike ________________ a shower tonight. (take)
마이크는 오늘밤 샤워를 할 것이다.

07 They ________________ a movie tomorrow. (watch)
그들은 내일 영화를 보지 않을 것이다.

08 My friends ________________ basketball. (play)
내 친구들은 농구를 할 것이다.

09 We ________________ pizza for lunch. (eat)
우리는 점심식사로 피자를 먹을 것이다.

10 We ________________ the house today. (clean)
우리는 오늘 집 청소를 하지 않을 것이다.

**Words**

☐ meet 만나다 ☐ visit 방문하다 ☐ cell phone 휴대전화(기) ☐ restaurant 식당
☐ shopping 쇼핑 ☐ weekend 주말 ☐ tonight 오늘밤(에) ☐ clean 청소하다

## 2 다음 우리말과 일치하도록 빈칸에 주어진 단어와 be going to 표현을 이용하여 쓰세요.

| make | wash | watch | visit | help |
|---|---|---|---|---|
| get up | play | read | study | invite |

01 Sarah ___is going to make___ a chocolate cake.
사라는 초콜릿 케이크를 만들 것이다.

02 I ____________________ the museum.
나는 박물관을 방문하지 않을 것이다.

03 Alice ____________________ him.
앨리스가 그를 도와줄 것이다.

04 I ____________________ my car.
나는 세차를 할 것이다.

05 She ____________________ at 7.
그녀는 7시에 일어날 것이다.

06 He ____________________ tennis this afternoon.
그는 오늘 오후에 테니스를 치지 않을 것이다.

07 We ____________________ math tomorrow.
우리는 내일 수학을 공부할 것이다.

08 ________ you ____________________ your friends?
당신은 친구들을 초대할 건가요?

09 ________ they ____________________ TV this afternoon?
그들은 오늘 오후 TV를 볼 건가요?

10 ________ he ____________________ the book?
그는 그 책을 읽을 건가요?

**Words**

☐ invite 초대하다 ☐ chocolate 초콜릿 ☐ museum 박물관 ☐ this afternoon 오늘 오후
☐ math 수학 ☐ tomorrow 내일

## 1 다음 우리말과 일치하도록 주어진 단어를 이용하여 빈칸에 알맞은 표현을 쓰세요.

**01** A: 당신은 자전거를 탈 건가요?
B: 예, 탈 거예요.
A: ___Are___ you going to ___ride___ a bike? (ride)
B: Yes, ___I___ ___am___.

**02** A: 당신은 설거지를 할 건가요?
B: 아니요, 하지 않을 거예요.
A: ________ you going to ________ the dishes? (wash)
B: No, ________ ________.

**03** A: 당신의 친구들은 농구를 할 건가요?
B: 아니요, 하지 않을 거예요.
A: ________ your friends going to ________ basketball? (play)
B: No, ________ ________.

**04** A: 그가 노래를 부를 건가요?
B: 예, 부를 거예요.
A: ________ he going to ________ a song? (sing)
B: Yes, ________ ________.

**05** A: 당신의 여동생은 친구들을 초대할 건가요?
B: 예, 초대할 거예요.
A: ________ your sister going to ________ her friends? (invite)
B: Yes, ________ ________.

**Words**
□ bike 자전거 □ ride 타다 □ wash 씻다, 닦다 □ basketball 농구 □ song 노래
□ invite 초대하다

## 2 다음 우리말과 일치하도록 주어진 단어를 이용해서 긍정문과 부정문을 완성하세요.

**01** 나는 피아노를 칠 것이다. (play)

➡ I ___am going to play___ the piano.

➡ 부정문 I ___am not going to play___ the piano.

**02** 그녀는 그 질문에 대답할 것이다. (answer)

➡ She ________________ the question.

➡ 부정문 She ________________ the question.

**03** 그는 그 방을 청소할 것이다. (clean)

➡ He ________________ the room.

➡ 부정문 He ________________ the room.

**04** 나의 친구들이 음악을 들을 것이다. (listen)

➡ My friends ________________ to music.

➡ 부정문 My friends ________________ to music.

**05** 그는 부산으로 이사 갈 것이다. (move)

➡ He ________________ to Busan.

➡ 부정문 He ________________ to Busan.

**06** 데이비드는 햄버거를 먹을 것이다. (eat)

➡ David ________________ a hamburger.

➡ 부정문 David ________________ a hamburger.

**07** 나의 삼촌은 피자를 만들 예정이다. (make)

➡ My uncle ________________ pizza.

➡ 부정문 My uncle ________________ pizza.

**Words**

- ☐ answer 대답하다 ☐ question 질문 ☐ clean 청소하다 ☐ music 음악
- ☐ move 이사 가다 ☐ hamburger 햄버거

## 1 다음 우리말과 일치하도록 빈칸에 보기의 단어와 can/can't를 이용하여 쓰세요.

| run | drive | help | solve | understand |
|---|---|---|---|---|
| swim | speak | ride | watch | move |

01 They ____can run____ fast.
그들은 빨리 달릴 수 있다.

02 I ____________ the word.
나는 그 단어를 이해할 수 있다.

03 My dad ____________ fast.
나의 아빠는 빨리 수영할 수 있다.

04 Tom ____________ three languages.
톰은 세 가지 언어를 말할 수 있다.

05 He ____________ a bike.
그는 자전거를 탈 수 없다.

06 You ____________ this movie.
너는 이 영화를 볼 수 없다.

07 We ____________ the table.
우리는 그 식탁을 옮길 수 있다.

08 I ____________ the problem.
나는 그 문제를 풀 수 없다.

09 She ____________ us.
그녀는 우리를 도와줄 수 없다.

10 David ____________ a car.
데이비드는 자동차를 운전할 수 없다.

**Words**

- □ understand 이해하다 □ move 옮기다 □ word 단어 □ language 언어
- □ movie 영화 □ problem 문제

## 2 다음 우리말과 일치하도록 주어진 단어와 be going to를 이용하여 쓰세요.

01 나는 7시에 TV를 볼 것이다. (watch)

➡ I ___am going to watch___ TV at 7.

02 그녀는 그것을 사지 않을 것이다. (buy)

➡ She ________________ it.

03 당신은 수원으로 이사 갈 건가요? (move)

➡ ________ you ________________ to Suwon?

04 그들은 장갑을 끼지 않을 것이다. (wear)

➡ They ________________ gloves.

05 캐빈은 중국어를 배울 것이다. (learn)

➡ Kevin ________________ Chinese.

06 그 소년들은 음악을 들을 것이다. (listen)

➡ The boys ________________ to music.

07 그녀는 한국을 방문할 건가요? (visit)

➡ ________ she ________________ Korea?

08 나의 언니들은 그 방을 청소하지 않을 것이다. (clean)

➡ My sisters ________________ the room.

09 그들은 영어를 공부할 것이다. (study)

➡ They ________________ English.

10 나는 설거지를 하지 않을 것이다. (wash)

➡ I ________________ the dishes.

**Words**

☐ watch 보다 ☐ buy 사다 ☐ glove 장갑 ☐ learn 배우다 ☐ music 음악

# Exercise CHAPTER 8

**1** 다음 중 빈칸에 들어갈 수 없는 것을 고르세요.

Tommy is going to ____________ you.

① meet ② help ③ teach
④ visits ⑤ call

[2-3] 다음 중 밑줄 친 부분이 잘못된 것을 고르세요.

**2**
① I can speak English.
② He can't plays the violin.
③ She can ride a bike.
④ We can make pizza.
⑤ They can't play baseball.

**3**
① I be going to read the book.
② She is going to buy the bag.
③ You are going to meet him.
④ It is going to be windy.
⑤ We are going to make pizza.

**4** 다음 중 빈칸에 들어갈 수 있는 것을 고르세요.

We are going to visit the museum ________.
우리는 ______ 박물관을 방문할 것이다.

① yesterday ② last week
③ last Sunday ④ tomorrow
⑤ last month

1.
[be going to+동사원형] 형태입니다.

3.
be동사(is, am, are)는 인칭이나 수에 따라 다르게 써야 합니다

4.
[be going to+동사원형]은 '~할 것이다'라는 의미로 미래에 할 일을 계획할 때 사용합니다.

## 5

다음 중 우리말과 일치하도록 빈칸에 들어갈 단어가 바르게 짝지어진 것을 고르세요.

- 나는 저 나무에 올라갈 수 있다.
  ➡ I ________ climb that tree.
- 그는 산책을 할 것이다.
  ➡ He ________ take a walk.

① can – be going to
② can't – is going to
③ can't – are going to
④ can – is going to
⑤ can – are going to

5.
**climb** 오르다
**take a walk** 산책하다

## 6

다음 중 문장을 부정문으로 바꿀 때 not이 들어갈 곳을 고르세요.

They ① are ② going ③ to ④ play ⑤ football.
그들은 미식축구를 할 것이다.

6.
**football** (미식)축구

## 7

다음 문장을 부정문으로 바꿔 쓰세요.

(1) He can ride a bike.

➡ ________________________________

(2) He is going to cook dinner.

➡ ________________________________

7.
can의 부정형은 can't입니다.
부정문은 be동사 다음에 not을 씁니다.

## 8

다음 문장을 의문문으로 바꿔 쓰세요.

(1) She can play the violin.

➡ ________________________________

(2) They are going to clean the classroom.

➡ ________________________________

다음 단어의 뜻을 쓰고, 단어를 더 써보세요.

| No. | Word | 뜻 | 쓰기 | No. | Word | 뜻 | 쓰기 |
|---|---|---|---|---|---|---|---|
| 01 | answer | 대답하다 | answer | 02 | chocolate | | |
| 03 | clean | | | 04 | climb | | |
| 05 | drive | | | 06 | enter | | |
| 07 | fishing | | | 08 | fix | | |
| 09 | football | | | 10 | French | | |
| 11 | glove | | | 12 | harp | | |
| 13 | invite | | | 14 | language | | |
| 15 | math | | | 16 | move | | |
| 17 | party | | | 18 | question | | |
| 19 | sea | | | 20 | solve | | |
| 21 | soon | | | 22 | start | | |
| 23 | tennis | | | 24 | tomorrow | | |
| 25 | tonight | | | 26 | truck | | |
| 27 | understand | | | 28 | weekend | | |
| 29 | win | | | 30 | word | | |

# 실전모의고사

실전모의고사 1회

실전모의고사 2회

실전모의고사 3회

# 실전모의고사 1회

3점 25문항
5점 5문항

**01** 다음 중 명사가 아닌 것을 고르세요.

① happy ② friend
③ teacher ④ apple
⑤ book

**02** 다음 중 형용사가 아닌 것을 고르세요.

① wonderful ② big
③ write ④ rich
⑤ happy

**03** 다음 중 빈칸에 들어갈 수 없는 것을 고르세요.

I need two ________.

① computers ② bags
③ books ④ apple
⑤ pencils

**04** 다음 중 빈칸에 an이 필요한 것을 고르세요.

① I'm _____ doctor.
② This is _____ apple.
③ This is _____ book.
④ She is _____ teacher.
⑤ I need _____ pencil.

**05** 다음 중 빈칸에 공통으로 들어갈 알맞은 것을 고르세요.

- It ________ a dog.
- She ________ in the classroom.

① be ② is
③ are ④ being
⑤ am

**06** 다음 중 빈칸에 들어갈 알맞은 것을 고르세요.

We are ______________.

① a student ② a students
③ doctors ④ a doctor
⑤ driver

**07** 다음 중 밑줄 친 부분이 잘못된 것을 고르세요.

① They are doctors.
② I'm a soldier.
③ It is a horse.
④ He is scientists.
⑤ She is a student.

**08** 다음 중 반대말끼리 짝지어지지 않은 것을 고르세요.

① rich - poor ② long - short
③ tall - big ④ strong - weak
⑤ hot - cold

**09** 다음 중 대화의 빈칸에 들어갈 알맞은 대답을 고르세요.

A: Are they doctors?
B: No, ________________.

① you aren't ② he isn't
③ it isn't ④ we aren't
⑤ they aren't

**10** 다음 중 어색한 문장을 고르세요.

① I'm not a doctor.
② He isn't a singer.
③ Is it a zebra?
④ We isn't pianists.
⑤ Are you a teacher?

**11** 다음 중 문장을 부정문으로 바르게 고친 것을 고르세요.

This story is funny.

① Not this story is funny.
② This not story is funny.
③ This story does not funny.
④ This story isn't funny.
⑤ This story not is funny.

**12** 다음 중 빈칸에 Is가 올 수 없는 것을 고르세요.

① _____ he your brother?
② _____ it a taxi?
③ _____ Sam in the classroom?
④ _____ she a pianist?
⑤ _____ they lions?

**13** 다음 중 대화의 빈칸에 들어갈 알맞은 대답을 고르세요.

A: Is your uncle a scientist?
B: No, ________________.

① he isn't ② he is
③ we are ④ she isn't
⑤ they aren't

**14** 다음 중 동사의 3인칭 단수형이 잘못된 것을 고르세요.

① walk - walks ② make - makes
③ work - works ④ stay - stays
⑤ do - dos

**15** 다음 중 밑줄 친 부분이 알맞은 것을 고르세요.

① We likes hamburgers.
② It eat grass.
③ The boy jump high.
④ My uncle works hard.
⑤ They likes pizza.

**16** 다음 중 빈칸에 들어갈 말이 순서대로 바르게 연결된 것을 고르세요.

• My brother _____ to school by bus.
• I _____ to school by bike.
• David _____ to school by subway.

① go - goes - goes
② go - go - goes
③ goes - goes - go
④ goes - go - goes
⑤ go - goes - go

17 다음 중 빈칸에 들어갈 수 없는 것을 고르세요.

Jane ________ chocolate.

① likes ② buy
③ eats ④ has
⑤ makes

18 다음 중 빈칸에 들어갈 말이 알맞은 것을 고르세요.

Tom ________ live in Korea.

① isn't ② aren't
③ do ④ don't
⑤ doesn't

19 다음 중 빈칸에 들어갈 말이 나머지와 다른 것을 고르세요.

① _______ he play the piano?
② _______ they learn English?
③ _______ the boys play basketball?
④ _______ your brothers like pizza?
⑤ _______ you like apple?

20 다음 중 밑줄 친 부분이 잘못된 것을 고르세요.

① She doesn't ask questions.
② We don't have a pet.
③ You don't study English.
④ They doesn't know me.
⑤ He doesn't drink milk.

[21-22] 다음 중 빈칸에 들어갈 수 없는 것을 고르세요.

21

It is ________ cat.

① my ② her
③ his ④ their
⑤ it

22

________ is a student.

① My sister ② Jane
③ He ④ She
⑤ Them

23 다음 중 빈칸에 공통으로 들어갈 말이 알맞은 것을 고르세요.

- Tom is ________ brother.
- He loves ________.

① our ② your
③ him ④ her
⑤ their

24 다음 중 빈칸에 들어갈 말이 알맞은 것을 고르세요.

The book is interesting. I read ______ every day.

① me ② her
③ him ④ them
⑤ it

25 다음 중 빈칸에 들어갈 수 없는 것을 고르세요.

I am going to ________ the car.

① buys ② wash
③ drive ④ sell
⑤ park

5점
26 다음 우리말을 영어로 옮긴 것 중 가장 알맞은 것을 고르세요.

당신은 내일 박물관을 방문할 건가요?

① Will you going to visit the museum tomorrow?
② Are you go to visit the museum tomorrow?
③ Are you going visit the museum tomorrow?
④ Are you going to visit the museum tomorrow?
⑤ Are you to visit the museum tomorrow?

5점
27 다음 우리말과 일치하도록 빈칸에 들어갈 알맞은 말을 쓰세요.

(1) I love ________ very much.
나는 그녀를 매우 사랑한다.

(2) She visits ________ every Sunday.
그녀는 매주 일요일 그들을 방문한다.

5점
28 다음 문장을 의문문으로 바꿔 쓰세요.

(1) You are a good student.
→ ________________

(2) Your brother likes math.
→ ________________

5점
29 다음 문장을 부정문으로 바꿔 쓰세요.

(1) We watch TV.
→ ________________

(2) My brother likes science.
→ ________________

(3) He can ride a bike.
→ ________________

5점
30 다음 우리말과 일치하도록 밑줄 친 부분을 바르게 고쳐 쓰세요.

He loves <u>him</u> parents.
그는 그의 부모님들을 사랑한다.

→ ________________

91-100 Excellent
81-90 Good
61-80 Not bad
60 이하 Try Again

# 실전모의고사 2회

3점 25문항
5점 5문항

**01** 다음 중 명사의 복수형이 올바르지 않은 것을 고르세요.

① apple - apples
② teacher - teachers
③ knife - knives
④ watch - watchs
⑤ bus - buses

**02** 다음 중 빈칸에 an이 필요한 것을 고르세요.

① I'm _______ doctor.
② This is _______ egg.
③ This is _______ tiger.
④ She is _______ student.
⑤ He is _______ kind.

**03** 다음 중 빈칸에 들어갈 알맞은 것을 고르세요.

They are _________.

① an apple ② teachers
③ a book ④ a doctor
⑤ milk

**04** 다음 중 밑줄 친 부분을 인칭대명사로 바르게 바꾼 것을 고르세요.

His sister is an actress.

① He ② She
③ We ④ They
⑤ It

**05** 다음 중 잘못된 문장을 고르세요.

① She is a teacher.
② I'm a student.
③ It is a computer.
④ He is a pianist.
⑤ They are a cat.

**06** 다음 중 밑줄 친 단어의 반대말을 고르세요.

I'm hungry.

① happy ② strong
③ slow ④ full
⑤ poor

**07** 다음 우리말을 영어로 옮긴 것 중 가장 알맞은 것을 고르세요.

그녀는 아름다운 소녀다.

① She is girl beautiful.
② She is a girl beautiful.
③ She is beautiful girl.
④ She is a beautiful girl.
⑤ She is beautiful girls.

**08** 다음 중 반대말끼리 짝지어지지 않은 것을 고르세요.

① dirty - clean ② small - big
③ tall - short ④ strong - rich
⑤ new - old

**09** 다음 중 대화의 빈칸에 들어갈 알맞은 대답을 고르세요.

A: Are you hungry?
B: ______________________.

① No, it isn't. ② Yes, it is.
③ No, he isn't. ④ No, they aren't.
⑤ Yes, I am.

**10** 다음 중 우리말과 일치하도록 빈칸에 들어갈 알맞은 것을 고르세요.

They ________ in the classroom.
그들은 교실에 있지 않다.

① am not ② is
③ is not ④ are
⑤ aren't

**11** 다음 중 잘못된 문장을 고르세요.

① I'm not a scientist.
② He isn't happy.
③ Is it a computer?
④ They isn't actors.
⑤ Is she a writer?

**12** 다음 중 빈칸에 Are를 쓸 수 없는 것을 고르세요.

① _______ your brothers tall?
② _______ they doctors?
③ _______ the boys in the gym?
④ _______ it a pen?
⑤ _______ you hungry?

**13** 다음 중 밑줄 친 부분이 잘못된 것을 고르세요.

① She plays computer games.
② Tom watches TV every day.
③ They work at a hospital.
④ She loves James.
⑤ We has five cats.

**14** 다음 중 동사가 아닌 것을 고르세요.

① eat ② like
③ walk ④ fast
⑤ cook

**15** 다음 중 빈칸에 들어갈 알맞은 것을 고르세요.

________ get up at 7.

① They
② The girl
③ My brother
④ Cindy
⑤ She

**16** 다음 중 동사의 3인칭 단수형이 잘못된 것을 고르세요.

① play - plays
② finish - finishs
③ help - helps
④ go - goes
⑤ study - studies

**17** 다음 중 빈칸에 들어갈 수 없는 것을 고르세요.

_________ don't like pizza.

① They ② He
③ The boys ④ We
⑤ The students

**18** 다음 중 밑줄 친 부분이 잘못된 것을 고르세요.

① He doesn't play the piano.
② We don't have a house.
③ She doesn't have a pencil.
④ They doesn't know me.
⑤ I don't like spaghetti.

**19** 다음 중 빈칸에 들어갈 말이 나머지와 다른 것을 고르세요.

① _______ they play the guitar?
② _______ you learn English?
③ _______ the boys watch TV?
④ _______ she like hamburgers?
⑤ _______ you like Korean food?

**20** 다음 중 대화의 빈칸에 들어갈 알맞은 대답을 고르세요.

A: Does Susie have a pet?
B: ____________________________

① Yes, she is.
② Yes, she doesn't.
③ No, she isn't.
④ No, she doesn't.
⑤ No, she does.

**21** 다음 우리말을 영어로 옮긴 것 중 가장 알맞은 것을 고르세요.

나의 언니들은 쇼핑하러 가지 않는다.

① My sisters go don't shopping.
② My sisters doesn't go shopping.
③ My sisters don't go shopping.
④ My sisters isn't go shopping.
⑤ My sisters aren't go shopping.

**22** 다음 중 빈칸에 들어갈 알맞은 것을 고르세요.

The students are in the classroom.
_________ are from Korea.

① It ② He
③ She ④ We
⑤ They

**23** 다음 중 빈칸에 들어갈 말이 차례대로 짝지어진 것을 고르세요.

_________ know _________.
_________ name is John.

① You - his - Him
② I - him - You
③ Me - him - His
④ We - him - His
⑤ Her - him - His

**24** 다음 중 밑줄 친 부분이 잘못된 것을 고르세요.

① I can speak Chinese.
② Jim can't play the violin.
③ She can't rides a horse.
④ We can make spaghetti.
⑤ I can do it.

**25** 다음 우리말을 영어로 옮긴 것 중 가장 알맞은 것을 고르세요.

그의 친구들은 그 파티에 올 수 없다.

① His friends can come to the party.
② His friends don't come to the party.
③ His friends can't come to the party.
④ His friends can't comes to the party.
⑤ His friends come can't to the party.

5점

**26** 다음 우리말과 일치하도록 빈칸에 알맞은 단어를 쓰세요.

그는 매일 그의 숙제를 한다.

→ He ________ his homework every day.

5점

**27** 다음 문장을 부정문과 의문문으로 바꿔 쓰세요.

Susan is a doctor.

(1) 부정문: ________________
(2) 의문문: ________________

5점

**28** 다음 주어진 문장을 보기처럼 바꿔 쓰세요.

It is a new bike. → The bike is new.

(1) It is an old watch.
→ ________________

(2) He is a brave man.
→ ________________

5점

**29** 다음 빈칸에 공통으로 들어갈 말을 쓰세요.

• Apples ________ delicious.
• They ________ my friends.

→ ________________

5점

**30** 다음 문장을 의문문으로 바꿔 쓰세요.

The girls like K-pop music.

→ ________________

91-100 Excellent
81-90 Good
61-80 Not bad
60 이하 Try Again

# 실전모의고사 3회

3점 25문항
5점 5문항

**01** 다음 중 밑줄 친 단어가 명사가 아닌 것을 고르세요.

① I love my parents.
② He is my friend.
③ My brother is kind.
④ I have a dog.
⑤ Tom is very tall.

**02** 다음 중 빈칸에 들어갈 수 없는 것을 고르세요.

She has four ______________.

① computers ② eraser
③ bags ④ dishes
⑤ cats

[03-04] 다음 중 우리말과 일치하도록 빈칸에 들어갈 알맞은 것을 고르세요.

**03**

This is a _________ car.
이것은 안전한 자동차다.

① good ② safe
③ happy ④ fast
⑤ interesting

**04**

They are _________ shoes.
그것들은 더러운 신발들이다.

① strong ② make
③ old ④ pretty
⑤ dirty

**05** 다음 중 대화의 빈칸에 들어갈 알맞은 대답을 고르세요.

A: Is she smart?
B: ____________________________

① Yes, I am. ② Yes, he is.
③ Yes, you are. ④ Yes, she is.
⑤ Yes, they are.

**06** 다음 중 형용사 strong이 들어갈 위치로 알맞은 것을 고르세요.

① Tom ② is ③ a ④ boy ⑤.

**07** 다음 중 형용사가 아닌 것을 고르세요.

① strong ② make
③ old ④ clean
⑤ rich

**08** 다음 중 잘못된 문장을 고르세요.

① She is a dentist.
② We are scientists.
③ She is soccer players.
④ Tom is a good student.
⑤ You are doctors.

**09** 다음 중 인칭대명사의 성격이 다른 것을 고르세요?

① them ② she
③ he ④ I
⑤ we

**10** 다음 중 대화의 빈칸에 들어갈 알맞은 대답을 고르세요.

A: Is your mother a housewife?
B: Yes, ______________.

① I am ② he is
③ she is ④ they are
⑤ we are

**11** 다음 중 두 단어의 관계가 다른 것을 고르세요.

① I - my
② she - her
③ we - us
④ they - their
⑤ he - his

**12** 다음 중 빈칸에 들어갈 수 없는 것을 고르세요.

They are ______________ friends.

① my ② his
③ her ④ our
⑤ them

**13** 다음 중 밑줄 친 부분을 대신하는 말을 고르세요.

She likes the boy.
→ She likes ______________.

① me ② him
③ her ④ our
⑤ them

**14** 다음 중 밑줄 친 부분이 잘못된 것을 고르세요.

① She washes her face.
② Jim likes apples.
③ The babies cries at night.
④ He teaches English.
⑤ I eat lunch at noon.

**15** 다음 중 빈칸에 들어갈 알맞은 것을 고르세요.

We ______________ dinner at 7.

① likes ② makes
③ eats ④ have
⑤ has

**16** 다음 중 밑줄 친 부분이 잘못된 것을 고르세요.

① He doesn't eat breakfast.
② They don't have computers.
③ We don't learn English.
④ They don't know me.
⑤ I don't has coins.

[17-18] 다음 중 빈칸에 들어갈 수 없는 것을 고르세요.

**17**

_______ plays basketball every day.

① Tom ② The girl
③ My brother ④ I
⑤ She

**18**

Do _______ like ice cream?

① they ② your mother
③ the boys ④ you
⑤ your friends

**19** 다음 중 빈칸에 들어갈 알맞은 말을 고르세요.

The movie is very interesting. I watch _______ every day.

① it ② them
③ you ④ him
⑤ her

**20** 다음 중 우리말과 일치하도록 빈칸에 들어갈 말이 바르게 짝지어진 것을 고르세요.

It isn't _______ book. It is _______ book.
그것은 나의 책이 아니다. 그것은 그의 책이다.

① your - her ② your - their
③ my - his ④ his - their
⑤ my - her

**21** 다음 중 밑줄 친 부분이 잘못된 것을 고르세요.

① I eat <u>them</u> every day.
② I don't know <u>her</u> name.
③ He loves <u>his</u> brother.
④ Tom visits <u>her</u> after school.
⑤ She doesn't have <u>me</u> pencil.

**22** 다음 우리말을 영어로 옮긴 것 중 가장 알맞은 것을 고르세요.

나는 내일 그들을 방문할 것이다.

① I can visit them tomorrow.
② I can't visit them tomorrow.
③ I'm going visit them tomorrow.
④ I'm go to visit them tomorrow.
⑤ I'm going to visit them tomorrow.

**23** 다음 중 밑줄 친 부분이 잘못된 것을 고르세요.

① I can't <u>play</u> the piano.
② He can <u>speaks</u> English.
③ They are going to <u>play</u> soccer.
④ We are not going to <u>play</u> tennis.
⑤ He can <u>move</u> the box.

**24** 다음 중 대화의 빈칸에 들어갈 알맞은 대답을 고르세요.

A: Can your friends speak English?
B: Yes, _______________.

① he can ② she can
③ I can ④ they can
⑤ we can

**25** 다음 중 두 문장이 비슷한 의미를 갖도록 빈칸에 알맞은 것을 고르세요.

I am going to meet her tomorrow.
→ I ________ meet her tomorrow.

① will ② can
③ do ④ does
⑤ going

5점
**26** 다음 문장을 부정문으로 바꿔 쓰세요.

(1) My mom works at a hospital.
→ ____________________

(2) He can play the guitar.
→ ____________________

5점
**27** 다음 밑줄 친 부분을 바르게 고쳐 쓰세요.

(1) I have five glass.
→ ____________________

(2) He drink milk in the morning.
→ ____________________

5점
**28** 다음 대화의 빈칸에 들어갈 알맞은 대답을 쓰세요.

A: Is the man diligent?
B: Yes, ____________.

→ ____________________

5점
**29** 다음 빈칸에 들어갈 알맞은 말을 쓰세요.

Jane and Tom are my cousins. I love ________.

→ ____________________

5점
**30** 다음 문장을 의문문으로 바꿔 쓰세요.

(1) She is going to buy the bag.
→ ____________________

(2) He can wash the dishes.
→ ____________________

| | |
|---|---|
| 91-100 | Excellent |
| 81-90 | Good |
| 61-80 | Not bad |
| 60 이하 | Try Again |

memo

Longman

# GRAMMAR MENTOR JOY

# WORKBOOK

EARLY START 1

Longman

# GRAMMAR MENTOR JOY

## WORKBOOK

EARLY START 1

# CHAPTER 1

## 1 다음 명사의 뜻을 쓰세요.

| 단어 | | 뜻 | 단어 | | 뜻 |
|---|---|---|---|---|---|
| 01 | teacher | 선생님 | 02 | ant | |
| 03 | doctor | | 04 | elephant | |
| 05 | student | | 06 | bag | |
| 07 | friend | | 08 | girl | |
| 09 | zoo | | 10 | boy | |
| 11 | school | | 12 | restaurant | |
| 13 | park | | 14 | watch | |
| 15 | book | | 16 | computer | |
| 17 | camera | | 18 | lion | |
| 19 | cat | | 20 | tiger | |
| 21 | chair | | 22 | cow | |
| 23 | zebra | | 24 | flower | |

## 2 다음 명사 앞에 a/an을 쓰고, 명사의 뜻을 쓰세요.

01 __a__ zoo → 동물원

02 ____ restaurant → ____________

03 ____ elephant → ____________

04 ____ camera → ____________

05 ____ ant → ____________

06 ____ singer → ____________

07 ____ hospital → ____________

08 ____ uncle → ____________

09 ____ girl → ____________

10 ____ doctor → ____________

11 ____ igloo → ____________

12 ____ airplane → ____________

# CHAPTER 1

## 1 다음 명사의 복수형을 쓰세요.

| | 단어 | 복수형 | | 단어 | 복수형 |
|---|---|---|---|---|---|
| 01 | girl | girls | 02 | brush | |
| 03 | bed | | 04 | lamp | |
| 05 | shoe | | 06 | picture | |
| 07 | class | | 08 | dish | |
| 09 | book | | 10 | box | |
| 11 | table | | 12 | bus | |
| 13 | brother | | 14 | bench | |
| 15 | church | | 16 | dog | |
| 17 | monkey | | 18 | tiger | |
| 19 | cup | | 20 | wife | |
| 21 | thief | | 22 | camera | |
| 23 | shirt | | 24 | fox | |

**2** 다음 명사 앞에 a/an을 쓰고, 명사의 뜻을 쓰세요. (a/an을 쓸 수 없는 곳에는 ×표 하세요.)

01 __×__ tigers → 호랑이들

02 ____ dolls → ________

03 ____ elephant → ________

04 ____ pencils → ________

05 ____ leaves → ________

06 ____ cat → ________

07 ____ foxes → ________

08 ____ umbrellas → ________

09 ____ onions → ________

10 ____ eraser → ________

11 ____ oranges → ________

12 ____ buses → ________

# REview TEST

## 1 다음 괄호 안에 알맞은 것에 동그라미 하고, 명사의 뜻을 쓰세요.

01 ( a / (an) ) apple → 사과

02 ( a / an ) baby → ____________

03 ( a / an ) glass → ____________

04 ( a / an ) email → ____________

05 ( a / an ) telephone → ____________

06 ( a / an ) friend → ____________

07 ( a / an ) album → ____________

08 ( a / an ) bottle → ____________

09 ( a / an ) zebra → ____________

10 ( a / an ) onion → ____________

11 ( a / an ) artist → ____________

12 ( a / an ) bridge → ____________

## 2 다음 밑줄 친 부분을 바르게 고쳐 쓰세요. (고칠 필요가 없는 곳에는 ○표 하세요.)

01 I have three dog. → dogs
나는 개가 세 마리 있다.

02 I have a book. → ______
나는 책이 한 권 있다.

03 I have four apple. → ______
나는 사과가 네 개 있다.

04 I have five dish. → ______
나는 접시가 다섯 개 있다.

05 I have two brush. → ______
나는 붓이 두 개 있다.

06 I have three doll. → ______
나는 인형이 세 개 있다.

07 I have three knife. → ______
나는 칼이 세 개 있다.

08 I have two brother. → ______
나는 형제가 두 명 있다.

09 I have a sister. → ______
나는 언니가 한 명 있다.

10 I have a radio. → ______
나는 라디오가 한 개 있다.

# Vocabulary TEST

| | 단어 | 뜻 |
|---|---|---|
| 01 | airplane | 비행기 |
| 02 | ant | 개미 |
| 03 | bench | 벤치 |
| 04 | brush | 붓 |
| 05 | church | 교회 |
| 06 | class | 수업 |
| 07 | computer | 컴퓨터 |
| 08 | dish | 접시 |
| 09 | doctor | 의사 |
| 10 | doll | 인형 |
| 11 | elephant | 코끼리 |
| 12 | flower | 꽃 |
| 13 | fox | 여우 |
| 14 | hospital | 병원 |
| 15 | igloo | 이글루 |

| | 단어 | 뜻 |
|---|---|---|
| 16 | knife | 칼 |
| 17 | lamp | 램프, 등 |
| 18 | leaf | 나뭇잎 |
| 19 | lion | 사자 |
| 20 | monkey | 원숭이 |
| 21 | park | 공원 |
| 22 | picture | 그림, 사진 |
| 23 | restaurant | 식당 |
| 24 | singer | 가수 |
| 25 | student | 학생 |
| 26 | thief | 도둑 |
| 27 | umbrella | 우산 |
| 28 | wife | 아내 |
| 29 | zebra | 얼룩말 |
| 30 | zoo | 동물원 |

## 1 다음 우리말 뜻에 해당하는 영어 단어를 쓰세요.

01 비행기 ➡ airplane
02 나뭇잎 ➡ ______
03 동물원 ➡ ______
04 벤치 ➡ ______
05 꽃 ➡ ______
06 접시 ➡ ______
07 도둑 ➡ ______
08 원숭이 ➡ ______
09 학생 ➡ ______
10 병원 ➡ ______
11 붓 ➡ ______
12 인형 ➡ ______
13 공원 ➡ ______
14 이글루 ➡ ______
15 그림, 사진 ➡ ______
16 우산 ➡ ______

## 2 다음 영어 단어에 해당하는 우리말 뜻을 쓰세요.

01 computer ➡ 컴퓨터
02 singer ➡ ______
03 zebra ➡ ______
04 knife ➡ ______
05 ant ➡ ______
06 class ➡ ______
07 church ➡ ______
08 fox ➡ ______
09 restaurant ➡ ______
10 lamp ➡ ______
11 wife ➡ ______
12 lion ➡ ______
13 elephant ➡ ______
14 doctor ➡ ______

# CHAPTER 2

## 1 다음 괄호 안에서 알맞은 be동사를 고르세요.

01 He ( am / is / are ) an actor. 그는 배우다.

02 It ( am / is / are ) heavy. 그것은 무겁다.

03 You ( am / is / are ) my friends. 너희들은 내 친구들이다.

04 We ( am / is / are ) students. 우리는 학생들이다.

05 They ( am / is / are ) inventors. 그들은 발명가들이다.

06 You ( am / is / are ) pretty. 너는 예쁘다.

07 I ( am / is / are ) a painter. 나는 화가다.

08 It ( am / is / are ) a knife. 그것은 칼이다.

09 They ( am / is / are ) albums. 그것들은 앨범들이다.

10 He ( am / is / are ) a singer. 그는 가수다.

11 She ( am / is / are ) a model. 그녀는 모델이다.

12 He ( am / is / are ) smart. 그는 영리하다.

## 2 다음 밑줄 친 부분을 줄임말을 이용해서 다시 쓰세요.

01 We are students. → We're students.
우리는 학생들이다.

02 They are actors. → ________ actors.
그들은 배우들이다.

03 He is a doctor. → ________ a doctor.
그는 의사다.

04 It is a dog. → ________ a dog.
그것은 개다.

05 We are happy. → ________ happy.
우리는 행복하다.

06 I am hungry. → ________ hungry.
나는 배가 고프다.

07 She is short. → ________ short.
그녀는 키가 작다.

08 They are policemen. → ________ policemen.
그들은 경찰관들이다.

09 You are a designer. → ________ a designer.
너는 디자이너다.

10 We are dancers. → ________ dancers.
우리는 무용수들이다.

11 It is a blender. → ________ a blender.
그것은 믹서다.

12 She is a writer. → ________ a writer.
그녀는 작가다.

# CHAPTER 2

## 1 다음 우리말과 일치하도록 괄호 안에서 알맞은 것을 고르세요.

01 They are ( a doctor / doctors ). 그들은 의사들이다.

02 You're ( an actress / actresses ). 너는 여배우다.

03 We are ( a cook / cooks ). 우리는 요리사들이다.

04 They are ( a vase / vases ). 그것들은 꽃병들이다.

05 It's ( a fan / fans ). 그것은 부채다.

06 ( It is / They are ) a toy. 그것은 장난감이다.

07 I'm in the ( garage / playground ). 나는 차고에 있다.

08 He is in the ( room / gym ). 그는 체육관에 있다.

09 They're on the ( library / street ). 그들은 거리에 있다.

10 She's in the ( garden / classroom ). 그녀는 정원에 있다.

11 ( She is / We are ) a baseball player. 그녀는 야구 선수다.

12 ( She is / They are ) fashion models. 그들은 패션모델들이다.

## 2 다음 빈칸에 우리말을 써서 완성하세요.

01 He is a pilot. → 그는 (비행기) 조종사다 .

02 You are a nurse. → 너는 ____________ .

03 It's a storybook. → 그것은 ____________ .

04 I'm in the gym. → 나는 ____________ .

05 We are in the library. → 우리는 ____________ .

06 You're artists. → 너희들은 ____________ .

07 Mom is in the kitchen. → 엄마는 ____________ .

08 They are lemons. → 그것들은 ____________ .

09 He's a lawyer. → 그는 ____________ .

10 It's in the pot. → 그것은 ____________ .

11 She's in Seoul. → 그녀는 ____________ .

12 It's an umbrella. → 그것은 ____________ .

# REview TEST

**1** 다음 빈칸에 알맞은 인칭대명사나 be동사를 쓰세요.

01 그녀는 앤이다. → ___She___ is Anne.

02 그는 학생이다. → He ________ a student.

03 그것들은 동물들이다. → They ________ animals.

04 그것은 자전거다. → ________ is a bicycle.

05 그들은 나의 삼촌들이다. → ________ are my uncles.

06 너희들은 나의 친구들이다. → You ________ my friends.

07 그는 경찰관이다. → ________ is a policeman.

08 그녀는 디자이너다. → She ________ a designer.

09 우리는 변호사들이다. → ________ are lawyers.

10 그것들은 바구니들이다. → They ________ baskets.

11 너희들은 매우 용감하다. → ________ are very brave.

12 나는 건강하다. → ________ am healthy.

## 2 다음 영어 문장을 우리말로 쓰세요.

01 It's a newspaper.

➡ 그것은 신문이다.

02 She's in the gym.

➡ ______________________

03 They are telephones.

➡ ______________________

04 He's Korean.

➡ ______________________

05 They are doctors.

➡ ______________________

06 They are stones.

➡ ______________________

07 We are singers.

➡ ______________________

08 It's an octopus.

➡ ______________________

09 We are in the building.

➡ ______________________

10 They are in the pot.

➡ ______________________

# Vocabulary TEST

| | 단어 | 뜻 |
|---|---|---|
| 01 | actress | 여배우 |
| 02 | album | 앨범 |
| 03 | artist | 예술가 |
| 04 | basket | 바구니 |
| 05 | blender | 믹서 |
| 06 | cook | 요리사 |
| 07 | dancer | 무용수 |
| 08 | designer | 디자이너 |
| 09 | doctor | 의사 |
| 10 | fan | 부채 |
| 11 | fashion | 패션 |
| 12 | garage | 차고 |
| 13 | garden | 정원 |
| 14 | gym | 체육관 |
| 15 | heavy | 무거운 |

| | 단어 | 뜻 |
|---|---|---|
| 16 | hungry | 배고픈 |
| 17 | inventor | 발명가 |
| 18 | lawyer | 변호사 |
| 19 | library | 도서관 |
| 20 | model | 모델 |
| 21 | painter | 화가 |
| 22 | policeman | 경찰관 |
| 23 | pot | 냄비 |
| 24 | pretty | 예쁜 |
| 25 | smart | 영리한 |
| 26 | stone | 돌 |
| 27 | storybook | 이야기책 |
| 28 | street | 거리 |
| 29 | toy | 장난감 |
| 30 | vase | 꽃병 |

## 1 다음 우리말 뜻에 해당하는 영어 단어를 쓰세요.

01 패션 → fashion
02 영리한 → ______
03 앨범 → ______
04 거리 → ______
05 경찰관 → ______
06 디자이너 → ______
07 변호사 → ______
08 예술가 → ______
09 의사 → ______
10 배고픈 → ______
11 돌 → ______
12 여배우 → ______
13 발명가 → ______
14 화가 → ______
15 부채 → ______
16 요리사 → ______

## 2 다음 영어 단어에 해당하는 우리말 뜻을 쓰세요.

01 garage → 차고
02 garden → ______
03 pretty → ______
04 basket → ______
05 vase → ______
06 blender → ______
07 pot → ______
08 model → ______
09 dancer → ______
10 storybook → ______
11 gym → ______
12 toy → ______
13 library → ______
14 heavy → ______

# CHAPTER 3

**1** 다음 형용사나 형용사의 뜻을 써서 표를 완성하세요.

| 단어 | | 뜻 | 단어 | | 뜻 |
|---|---|---|---|---|---|
| 01 | beautiful | 아름다운 | 02 | | 키가 큰, 높은 |
| 03 | ugly | | 04 | | (길이가) 긴 |
| 05 | clean | | 06 | | 키가 작은, 짧은 |
| 07 | | 낡은, 오래된 | 08 | round | |
| 09 | | 어린, 젊은 | 10 | square | |
| 11 | | 더러운 | 12 | happy | |
| 13 | big | | 14 | sad | |
| 15 | small | | 16 | hungry | |
| 17 | hot | | 18 | tired | |
| 19 | cold | | 20 | angry | |
| 21 | cloudy | | 22 | sleepy | |
| 23 | | 분홍색의 | 24 | sunny | |

## 2 다음 영어 표현을 우리말로 쓰세요.

01 a strong man → 강한 남자

02 a red ink → ____________

03 a hungry boy → ____________

04 a yellow brick → ____________

05 a small cat → ____________

06 a dirty house → ____________

07 a long snake → ____________

08 a blue jacket → ____________

09 a happy birthday → ____________

10 a short name → ____________

11 a clean towel → ____________

12 a kind doctor → ____________

# CHAPTER 3

## 1 다음 형용사의 반대말과 뜻을 쓰세요.

01 early 이른 → late 늦은

02 ugly 추한, 못생긴 → ____ ____

03 hungry 배고픈 → ____ ____

04 big 큰 → ____ ____

05 clean 깨끗한 → ____ ____

06 rich 부유한 → ____ ____

07 strong 강한 → ____ ____

08 long 긴 → ____ ____

09 old 오래된, 낡은 → ____ ____

10 tall 키가 큰 → ____ ____

11 hot 뜨거운 → ____ ____

12 fast 빠른 → ____ ____

## 2 다음 빈칸에 반대 의미가 되도록 문장을 완성하세요.

01 The computer is old. 그 컴퓨터는 오래되었다.
➡ The computer ___is new___. 그 컴퓨터는 새것이다.

02 She is a rich singer. 그녀는 부유한 가수다.
➡ She is ______________. 그녀는 가난한 가수다.

03 The cake is big. 그 케이크는 크다.
➡ The cake ______________. 그 케이크는 작다.

04 He is a strong man. 그는 강한 남자다.
➡ He is ______________. 그는 약한 남자다.

05 I am hungry. 나는 배가 고프다.
➡ I ______________. 나는 배가 부르다.

06 It is a clean towel. 그것은 깨끗한 수건이다.
➡ It is ______________. 그것은 더러운 수건이다.

07 The cat is beautiful. 그 고양이는 아름답다.
➡ The cat ______________. 그 고양이는 못생겼다.

08 She is a tall model. 그녀는 키가 큰 모델이다.
➡ She is ______________. 그녀는 키가 작은 모델이다.

09 The train is fast. 그 기차는 빠르다.
➡ The train ______________. 그 기차는 느리다.

10 The coffee is hot. 그 커피는 뜨겁다.
➡ The coffee ______________. 그 커피는 차갑다.

# REview TEST

**1** 다음 우리말과 일치하도록 빈칸에 보기의 단어를 이용하여 문장을 완성하세요.

| new | easy | yellow | kind | round |
|---|---|---|---|---|
| soft | lazy | nice | tired | strong |

01 It's a ___new___ book. 그것은 새 책이다.

02 He's a __________ man. 그는 친절한 남자다.

03 The table is __________. 그 식탁은 둥글다.

04 It's a __________ bed. 그것은 부드러운 침대다.

05 The man is __________. 그 남자는 게으르다.

06 They are __________ flowers. 그것들은 노란색 꽃들이다.

07 The student is __________. 그 학생은 피곤하다.

08 The car is __________. 그 자동차는 멋지다.

09 She's a __________ woman. 그녀는 강한 여자다.

10 It's an __________ problem. 그것은 쉬운 문제다.

## 2 다음 우리말과 일치하도록 주어진 단어들을 이용하여 문장을 완성하세요. (필요하면 a나 an을 넣으세요.)

01 그 자전거는 새것이다. (new)

➡ The bike ______is new______.

02 그 화가는 영리하다. (smart)

➡ The painter ____________________.

03 그것은 비싼 드레스다. (expensive / dress)

➡ It's ____________________.

04 나는 빨간 사과를 가지고 있다. (red / apple)

➡ I have ____________________.

05 그것은 정사각형의 식탁이다. (square / table)

➡ It's ____________________.

06 그녀는 긴 치마를 가지고 있다. (long / skirt)

➡ She has ____________________.

07 그것들은 높은 건물들이다. (tall / buildings)

➡ They are ____________________.

08 그것은 큰 가방이다. (big / bag)

➡ It's ____________________.

09 그 문제는 어렵다. (difficult)

➡ The problem ____________________.

10 그 답은 맞다. (right)

➡ The answer ____________________.

# Vocabulary TEST

| | 단어 | 뜻 |
|---|---|---|
| 01 | angry | 화가 난 |
| 02 | beautiful | 아름다운 |
| 03 | blue | 파란(색의) |
| 04 | brick | 벽돌 |
| 05 | building | 건물 |
| 06 | car | 자동차 |
| 07 | clean | 깨끗한 |
| 08 | cloudy | 흐린 |
| 09 | dirty | 더러운 |
| 10 | early | 이른, 일찍 |
| 11 | happy | 행복한 |
| 12 | ink | 잉크 |
| 13 | jacket | 자켓 |
| 14 | lazy | 게으른 |
| 15 | old | 낡은, 오래된 |

| | 단어 | 뜻 |
|---|---|---|
| 16 | painter | 화가 |
| 17 | problem | 문제 |
| 18 | round | 둥근 |
| 19 | sad | 슬픈 |
| 20 | sleepy | 졸린 |
| 21 | soft | 부드러운 |
| 22 | square | 정사각형의 |
| 23 | strong | 강한 |
| 24 | sunny | 맑은 |
| 25 | tired | 피곤한 |
| 26 | towel | 수건 |
| 27 | train | 기차 |
| 28 | ugly | 못생긴 |
| 29 | yellow | 노란(색의) |
| 30 | young | 어린, 젊은 |

## 1 다음 우리말 뜻에 해당하는 영어 단어를 쓰세요.

01 피곤한 ➡ tired
02 깨끗한 ➡ ____
03 낡은, 오래된 ➡ ____
04 맑은 ➡ ____
05 슬픈 ➡ ____
06 기차 ➡ ____
07 정사각형의 ➡ ____
08 이른, 일찍 ➡ ____
09 흐린 ➡ ____
10 둥근 ➡ ____
11 벽돌 ➡ ____
12 화가 난 ➡ ____
13 어린, 젊은 ➡ ____
14 부드러운 ➡ ____
15 노란(색의) ➡ ____
16 건물 ➡ ____

## 2 다음 영어 단어에 해당하는 우리말 뜻을 쓰세요.

01 lazy ➡ 게으른
02 blue ➡ ____
03 towel ➡ ____
04 ink ➡ ____
05 jacket ➡ ____
06 sleepy ➡ ____
07 strong ➡ ____
08 beautiful ➡ ____
09 painter ➡ ____
10 dirty ➡ ____
11 ugly ➡ ____
12 problem ➡ ____
13 happy ➡ ____
14 car ➡ ____

# CHAPTER 4

## 1 다음 문장을 부정문으로 바꿔 쓰세요. (축약형을 쓰지 마세요.)

01 They are bears. 그것들은 곰들이다.

➡ They are not bears.

02 The boy is strong. 그 소년은 강하다.

➡ ______________________

03 It is an orange. 그것은 오렌지다.

➡ ______________________

04 It is a new museum. 그것은 새 박물관이다.

➡ ______________________

05 The water is hot. 그 물은 뜨겁다.

➡ ______________________

06 The girls are in the playground. 그 소녀들은 운동장에 있다.

➡ ______________________

07 He is in the restaurant. 그는 식당에 있다.

➡ ______________________

08 The computers are silver. 그 컴퓨터들은 은색이다.

➡ ______________________

09 Lions are at the zoo. 사자들은 동물원에 있다.

➡ ______________________

10 You are hockey players. 너희들은 하키 선수들이다.

➡ ______________________

## 2 다음 문장을 부정문으로 만드세요. (축약형으로 만드세요.)

01 He is an artist. 그는 예술가다.

➡ He isn't an artist.

02 She is a fashion model. 그녀는 패션모델이다.

➡ ______________________

03 We are happy. 우리는 행복하다.

➡ ______________________

04 You are handsome. 너는 잘생겼다.

➡ ______________________

05 They are my students. 그들은 나의 학생들이다.

➡ ______________________

06 The baby is sleepy. 그 아기는 졸리다.

➡ ______________________

07 The ants are small. 그 개미들은 작다.

➡ ______________________

08 We are in the library. 우리는 도서관에 있다.

➡ ______________________

09 They are plates. 그것들은 접시들이다.

➡ ______________________

10 The player is in the hospital. 그 선수는 병원에 있다.

➡ ______________________

# CHAPTER 4

## 1 다음 문장을 의문문으로 바꿔 쓰세요.

01 She is in the garden. 그녀는 정원에 있다.

→ ___Is she___ in the garden?

02 Kate is smart. 케이트는 영리하다.

→ ______________ smart?

03 They are notebooks. 그것들은 공책들이다.

→ ______________ notebooks?

04 The coffee is hot. 그 커피는 뜨겁다.

→ ______________ hot?

05 The girls are in the bakery. 그 소녀들은 빵집에 있다.

→ ______________ in the bakery?

06 The actor is handsome. 그 배우는 잘생겼다.

→ ______________ handsome?

07 Tigers are in the forest. 호랑이들은 숲에 있다.

→ ______________ in the forest?

08 The bike is red. 그 자전거는 빨간색이다.

→ ______________ red?

09 He is a lazy student. 그는 게으른 학생이다.

→ ______________ a lazy student?

10 You are doctors. 너희들은 의사들이다.

→ ______________ doctors?

## 2 다음 대화의 빈칸에 들어갈 알맞은 대답을 쓰세요.

01 A: Is she in the kitchen? 그녀는 부엌에 있나요?
B: Yes, ______she is______.

02 A: Are you cold? 당신은 춥나요?
B: Yes, ____________.

03 A: Is the woman old? 그 여자는 나이가 많나요?
B: No, ____________.

04 A: Is it a laptop computer? 그것은 노트북 컴퓨터인가요?
B: Yes, ____________.

05 A: Are they programmers? 그들은 프로그래머들인가요?
B: No, ____________.

06 A: Am I stupid? 나는 어리석나요?
B: No, ____________.

07 A: Are you hungry? 당신은 배가 고픈가요?
B: No, ____________.

08 A: Are they your uncles? 그들은 당신의 삼촌들인가요?
B: Yes, ____________.

09 A: Is she your aunt? 그녀는 당신의 고모인가요?
B: No, ____________.

10 A: Are you strong? (복수형 주어) 당신들은 강한가요?
B: Yes, ____________.

# REview TEST

## 1 다음 우리말과 일치하도록 be동사와 주어진 단어를 이용하여 문장을 완성하세요.

01 그것들은 포도들이 아니다. 그것들은 레몬들이다. (grapes / lemons)

➡ They aren't grapes. They are lemons.

02 그것은 개구리가 아니다. 그것은 거북이다. (a frog / a turtle)

➡ It ____________. It ____________.

03 그것들은 당근들이 아니다. 그것들은 복숭아들이다. (carrots / peaches)

➡ They ____________. They ____________.

04 마이크는 아기가 아니다. 그는 소년이다. (a baby / a boy)

➡ Mike ____________. He ____________.

05 우리들은 형제가 아니다. 우리들은 친구들이다. (brothers / friends)

➡ We ____________. We ____________.

06 그녀는 학생이 아니다. 그녀는 선생님이다. (a student / a teacher)

➡ She ____________. She ____________.

07 나는 배가 고프지 않다. 나는 배가 부르다. (hungry / full)

➡ I ____________. I ____________.

08 그 책은 방에 있지 않다. 그것은 교실에 있다. (in the room / in the classroom)

➡ The book ____________. It ____________.

09 그 물은 차갑지 않다. 그것은 뜨겁다. (cold / hot)

➡ The water ____________. It ____________.

10 그 문제들은 어렵지 않다. 그것들은 쉽다. (difficult / easy)

➡ The problems ____________. They ____________.

## 2 다음 문장을 부정문과 의문문으로 바꿔 쓰세요.

01 They are in Seoul. 그들은 서울에 있다.

→ 부정문 They aren't in Seoul.

→ 의문문 Are they in Seoul?

02 She is a reporter. 그녀는 기자다.

→ 부정문 ______________________

→ 의문문 ______________________

03 You are in the park. 너는 공원에 있다.

→ 부정문 ______________________

→ 의문문 ______________________

04 The doctor is tall. 그 의사는 키가 크다.

→ 부정문 ______________________

→ 의문문 ______________________

05 The dog is fat. 그 개는 뚱뚱하다.

→ 부정문 ______________________

→ 의문문 ______________________

06 She is in the garage. 그녀는 차고에 있다.

→ 부정문 ______________________

→ 의문문 ______________________

07 They are in the yard. 그들은 마당에 있다.

→ 부정문 ______________________

→ 의문문 ______________________

# Vocabulary TEST

| | 단어 | 뜻 |
|---|---|---|
| 01 | bakery | 빵집 |
| 02 | bear | 곰 |
| 03 | bike | 자전거 |
| 04 | carrot | 당근 |
| 05 | coffee | 커피 |
| 06 | difficult | 어려운 |
| 07 | easy | 쉬운 |
| 08 | forest | 숲 |
| 09 | frog | 개구리 |
| 10 | grape | 포도 |
| 11 | handsome | 잘생긴 |
| 12 | hockey | 하키 |
| 13 | kitchen | 부엌 |
| 14 | lazy | 게으른 |
| 15 | lemon | 레몬 |

| | 단어 | 뜻 |
|---|---|---|
| 16 | museum | 박물관 |
| 17 | notebook | 공책 |
| 18 | orange | 오렌지 |
| 19 | peach | 복숭아 |
| 20 | plate | 접시 |
| 21 | playground | 운동장 |
| 22 | programmer | 프로그래머 |
| 23 | reporter | 기자 |
| 24 | silver | 은색(의) |
| 25 | stupid | 어리석은 |
| 26 | tiger | 호랑이 |
| 27 | turtle | 거북 |
| 28 | uncle | 삼촌 |
| 29 | water | 물 |
| 30 | yard | 마당 |

## 1 다음 우리말 뜻에 해당하는 영어 단어를 쓰세요.

01 어리석은 → stupid
02 공책 → ______
03 마당 → ______
04 박물관 → ______
05 당근 → ______
06 복숭아 → ______
07 삼촌 → ______
08 자전거 → ______
09 접시 → ______
10 물 → ______
11 어려운 → ______
12 부엌 → ______
13 게으른 → ______
14 은색(의) → ______
15 기자 → ______
16 오렌지 → ______

## 2 다음 영어 단어에 해당하는 우리말 뜻을 쓰세요.

01 handsome → 잘생긴
02 coffee → ______
03 bakery → ______
04 bear → ______
05 easy → ______
06 playground → ______
07 frog → ______
08 hockey → ______
09 turtle → ______
10 programmer → ______
11 forest → ______
12 lemon → ______
13 grape → ______
14 tiger → ______

# CHAPTER 5

**1** 다음 동사나 동사의 뜻을 써서 표를 완성하세요.

| | 단어 | 뜻 | | 단어 | 뜻 |
|---|---|---|---|---|---|
| 01 | eat | 먹다 | 02 | | 만들다 |
| 03 | sing | | 04 | | 뛰다, 점프하다 |
| 05 | study | | 06 | | 앉다 |
| 07 | need | | 08 | | 닦다, 솔질하다 |
| 09 | love | | 10 | | 휴대하다 |
| 11 | open | | 12 | | 날다 |
| 13 | draw | | 14 | | 놓치다,<br>그리워하다 |
| 15 | help | | 16 | | (글을) 쓰다 |
| 17 | buy | | 18 | | 밀다 |
| 19 | drink | | 20 | | 하다 |
| 21 | enjoy | | 22 | | 만나다 |
| 23 | catch | | 24 | | 놀다, 연주하다 |

## 2 다음 문장에서 동사에 동그라미 하고, 그 뜻을 쓰세요.

01 I (eat) an orange. → 먹다
나는 오렌지를 먹는다.

02 I sing a song. → ____________
나는 노래를 부른다.

03 We study English. → ____________
우리는 영어를 공부한다.

04 They need chairs. → ____________
그들은 의자들이 필요하다.

05 I love the novel. → ____________
나는 그 소설을 사랑한다.

06 They open the door. → ____________
그들은 그 문을 연다.

07 I draw pictures. → ____________
나는 그림들을 그린다.

08 I help the girl. → ____________
나는 그 소녀를 돕는다.

09 We buy apples. → ____________
우리는 사과들을 산다.

10 We drink milk. → ____________
우리는 우유를 마신다.

# CHAPTER 5

**1** 다음 괄호 안에서 주어가 3인칭 단수일 때 동사의 형태를 고르고, 단어의 뜻을 쓰세요.

01 enjoy ( enjoys / enjoyes ) → 즐기다

02 catch ( catches / catchs ) → ______

03 make ( makes / makies ) → ______

04 jump ( jumpes / jumps ) → ______

05 sit ( sits / sitts ) → ______

06 brush ( brushes / brushs ) → ______

07 carry ( carryes / carries ) → ______

08 fly ( flys / flies ) → ______

09 miss ( missies / misses ) → ______

10 write ( writes / writies ) → ______

11 push ( pushs / pushes ) → ______

12 do ( dos / does ) → ______

## 2 다음 괄호 안에서 알맞은 것을 고르세요.

01 She ( cook / cooks ) dinner at seven. 그녀는 7시에 저녁식사를 요리한다.

02 Dad ( wash / washes ) the dishes. 아빠가 설거지를 한다.

03 She ( go / goes ) to school every day. 그녀는 매일 학교에 간다.

04 They ( play / plays ) baseball after school. 그들은 방과 후 야구를 한다.

05 Mom ( walk / walks ) to the bus stop. 엄마는 버스정류장에 걸어간다.

06 She ( buys / buy ) apples at a market. 그녀는 시장에서 사과들을 산다.

07 The horse ( like / likes ) carrots. 그 말은 당근들을 좋아한다.

08 Sam ( have / has ) a bike. 샘은 자전거를 가지고 있다.

09 He ( do / does ) his homework after school. 그는 방과 후에 숙제를 한다.

10 Mary ( drink / drinks ) milk in the morning. 메리는 아침에 우유를 마신다.

11 The guest ( stay / stays ) at a hotel. 그 손님은 호텔에서 머문다.

12 She ( meet / meets ) Mike every day. 그녀는 매일 마이크를 만난다.

# REview TEST

**1** 다음 밑줄 친 부분을 바르게 고쳐 쓰세요.

01 The student fix the computer. → fixes
그 학생은 그 컴퓨터를 고친다.

02 We visits him every Friday. → ______
우리는 금요일마다 그를 방문한다.

03 We watches TV in the evening. → ______
우리는 저녁에 TV를 본다.

04 They plays basketball after school. → ______
그들은 방과 후에 농구를 한다.

05 Chris write in his diary every day. → ______
크리스는 매일 일기를 쓴다.

06 We has breakfast at 7 a.m. → ______
우리는 오전 7시에 아침을 먹는다.

07 I does my homework. → ______
나는 숙제를 한다.

08 She play the violin at the concert. → ______
그녀는 콘서트에서 바이올린을 연주한다.

09 They helps sick people. → ______
그들은 아픈 사람들을 돕는다.

10 She have big eyes. → ______
그녀는 큰 눈을 가지고 있다.

## 2 다음 주어진 단어를 이용해서 문장을 완성하세요.

01 톰은 방과 후에 축구를 한다. (play)

➡ Tom ___plays___ soccer after school.

02 그녀는 그녀의 담임 선생님을 그리워한다. (miss)

➡ She ____________ her homeroom teacher.

03 나의 사촌은 공원에서 산책한다. (take)

➡ My cousin ____________ a walk in the park.

04 그는 무대에서 노래를 부른다. (sing)

➡ He ____________ a song on the stage.

05 그 아기는 침대에서 잔다. (sleep)

➡ The baby ____________ on the bed.

06 그 소년은 오후에 우유를 마신다. (drink)

➡ The boy ____________ milk in the afternoon.

07 그 학생은 숙제를 한다. (do)

➡ The student ____________ his homework.

08 우리는 식사 후에 이를 닦는다. (brush)

➡ We ____________ our teeth after meals.

09 그들은 함께 점심식사를 한다. (have)

➡ They ____________ lunch together.

10 그 여자는 서울에 산다. (live)

➡ The woman ____________ in Seoul.

# Vocabulary TEST

| | 단어 | 뜻 |
|---|---|---|
| 01 | brush | 닦다, 솔질하다 |
| 02 | buy | 사다 |
| 03 | carry | 휴대하다 |
| 04 | catch | 잡다 |
| 05 | concert | 콘서트 |
| 06 | diary | 일기 |
| 07 | draw | 그리다 |
| 08 | eat | 먹다 |
| 09 | enjoy | 즐기다 |
| 10 | fix | 고치다 |
| 11 | guest | 손님 |
| 12 | help | 돕다 |
| 13 | homework | 숙제 |
| 14 | hotel | 호텔 |
| 15 | jump | 뛰다, 점프하다 |

| | 단어 | 뜻 |
|---|---|---|
| 16 | market | 시장 |
| 17 | meal | 식사 |
| 18 | meet | 만나다 |
| 19 | miss | 그리워하다 |
| 20 | need | 필요하다 |
| 21 | novel | 소설 |
| 22 | open | 열다 |
| 23 | people | 사람들 |
| 24 | push | 밀다 |
| 25 | sit | 앉다 |
| 26 | stage | 무대 |
| 27 | stay | 머무르다 |
| 28 | together | 함께 |
| 29 | visit | 방문하다 |
| 30 | write | 글을 쓰다 |

## 1 다음 우리말 뜻에 해당하는 영어 단어를 쓰세요.

01 함께 ➡ together
02 손님 ➡ ______
03 무대 ➡ ______
04 필요하다 ➡ ______
05 식사 ➡ ______
06 방문하다 ➡ ______
07 잡다 ➡ ______
08 만나다 ➡ ______
09 즐기다 ➡ ______
10 일기 ➡ ______
11 호텔 ➡ ______
12 글을 쓰다 ➡ ______
13 사람들 ➡ ______
14 뛰다, 점프하다 ➡ ______
15 콘서트 ➡ ______
16 닦다, 솔질하다 ➡ ______

## 2 다음 영어 단어에 해당하는 우리말 뜻을 쓰세요.

01 open ➡ 열다
02 carry ➡ ______
03 miss ➡ ______
04 buy ➡ ______
05 stay ➡ ______
06 sit ➡ ______
07 fix ➡ ______
08 eat ➡ ______
09 novel ➡ ______
10 help ➡ ______
11 market ➡ ______
12 draw ➡ ______
13 push ➡ ______
14 homework ➡ ______

# CHAPTER 6

## 1 다음 우리말과 일치하도록 빈칸에 알맞은 말을 쓰세요.

01 I ___don't___ go to school today.
나는 오늘 학교에 가지 않는다.

02 She __________ live in Seoul.
그녀는 서울에 살지 않는다.

03 They __________ play soccer.
그들은 축구를 하지 않는다.

04 My friend __________ go skating.
내 친구는 스케이트 타러 가지 않는다.

05 You __________ drink milk.
너는 우유를 마시지 않는다.

06 My sister __________ wear glasses.
내 누나는 안경을 쓰지 않는다.

07 The students __________ chat in class.
그 학생들은 수업 중에 이야기하지 않는다.

08 We __________ know him well.
우리는 그를 잘 알지 못한다.

09 The boy __________ open the window.
그 소년은 그 창문을 열지 않는다.

10 He __________ get up early.
그는 일찍 일어나지 않는다.

11 They __________ travel a lot.
그들은 여행을 많이 하지 않는다.

12 It __________ have a tail.
그것은 꼬리를 가지고 있지 않다.

**2** 다음 우리말과 일치하도록 보기의 단어를 이용하여 부정문을 완성하세요.
(단, **don't**나 **doesn't**를 쓰세요.)

| drive | like | speak | take |
|---|---|---|---|
| go | play | read | learn |

**01** He ___doesn't drive___ a truck.
그는 트럭을 운전하지 않는다.

**02** They ______________ to the library.
그들은 도서관에 가지 않는다.

**03** The girls ______________ hamburgers.
그 소녀들은 햄버거를 좋아하지 않는다.

**04** She ______________ a walk.
그녀는 산책을 하지 않는다.

**05** We ______________ basketball.
우리는 농구를 하지 않는다.

**06** Susan ______________ comic books.
수잔은 만화책을 읽지 않는다.

**07** The travelers ______________ English.
그 여행자들은 영어로 말하지 않는다.

**08** My brother ______________ math.
내 남동생은 수학을 배우지 않는다.

## 1 다음 우리말과 일치하도록 빈칸에 알맞은 말을 쓰세요.

01 ___Does___ it fly high?
그것은 하늘 높이 나나요?

02 ________ you live in New York?
당신들은 뉴욕에서 사나요?

03 ________ the boys play baseball?
그 소년들은 야구를 하나요?

04 ________ he take a walk?
그는 산책을 하나요?

05 ________ Jisu work at a bank?
지수는 은행에서 일하나요?

06 ________ they travel by train?
그들은 기차로 여행하나요?

07 ________ your brother clean his room?
당신 형은 그의 방을 청소하나요?

08 ________ the baby sleep well?
그 아기는 잘 자나요?

09 ________ the students do their homework?
그 학생들은 숙제를 하나요?

10 ________ Mark get up early?
마크는 일찍 일어나나요?

11 ________ he wear a cap?
그는 야구모자를 쓰나요?

12 ________ they have a pet?
그들은 애완동물이 있나요?

## 2 다음 우리말과 일치하도록 보기의 단어를 이용하여 의문문을 완성하세요. (단, 문장 앞에 **Do**나 **Does**를 쓰세요.)

| get up | watch | go | play |
|---|---|---|---|
| cook | have | work | study |

**01** ___Do___ you ___have___ an eraser?
당신은 지우개가 있나요?

**02** ________ they ________ the harp?
그들은 하프를 연주하나요?

**03** ________ she ________ early?
그녀는 일찍 일어나나요?

**04** ________ your mom ________ dinner?
당신 엄마가 저녁을 요리하나요?

**05** ________ his father ________ at a restaurant?
그의 아버지는 식당에서 일하나요?

**06** ________ Sam ________ TV at night?
샘은 밤에 TV를 보나요?

**07** ________ Ben and Cindy ________ shopping?
벤과 신디는 쇼핑을 가나요?

**08** ________ your sister ________ math?
당신 누나는 수학을 공부하나요?

# REview TEST

## 1 다음 문장을 부정문으로 바꿔 쓰세요.

01 Tom likes vegetables. 톰은 야채를 좋아한다.
→ Tom ______doesn't like vegetables______.

02 I listen to the radio. 나는 라디오를 듣는다.
→ I ____________________.

03 They clean their house. 그들은 그들의 집을 청소한다.
→ They ____________________.

04 The students study science. 그 학생들은 과학을 공부한다.
→ The students ____________________.

05 We go to school every day. 우리는 매일 학교에 간다.
→ We ____________________.

06 The baby sleeps well at night. 그 아기는 밤에 잘 잔다.
→ The baby ____________________.

07 My sister has long hair. 내 누나는 머리가 길다.
→ My sister ____________________.

08 The children play outside. 그 아이들은 밖에서 논다.
→ The children ____________________.

09 The man drives a car. 그 남자는 자동차를 운전한다.
→ The man ____________________.

10 It costs 100 dollars. 그것은 100달러다.
→ It ____________________.

## 2 다음 문장을 의문문으로 바꿔 쓰세요.

01 The boy goes to bed early. 그 소년은 일찍 자러 간다.

➡ Does the boy go to bed early?

02 He has a lot of money. 그는 많은 돈이 있다.

➡ ______________________________

03 She reads a newspaper every day. 그녀는 매일 신문을 읽는다.

➡ ______________________________

04 The children play soccer after school. 그 아이들은 방과 후에 축구를 한다.

➡ ______________________________

05 The woman works at a hospital. 그 여자는 병원에서 일한다.

➡ ______________________________

06 He brushes his teeth in the morning. 그는 아침에 양치를 한다.

➡ ______________________________

07 The students speak English. 그 학생들은 영어로 말한다.

➡ ______________________________

08 You write your name in Korean. 너는 한국어로 너의 이름을 쓴다.

➡ ______________________________

09 The store opens at 10. 그 상점은 10시에 문을 연다.

➡ ______________________________

10 The travelers visit the gallery. 그 여행자들은 미술관을 방문한다.

➡ ______________________________

# Vocabulary TEST

| | 단어 | 뜻 |
|---|---|---|
| 01 | cap | 야구모자 |
| 02 | chat | 이야기하다 |
| 03 | children | 아이들 |
| 04 | comic | 만화(의) |
| 05 | cook | 요리하다 |
| 06 | cost | (값이) ~이다 |
| 07 | dollar | 달러 |
| 08 | gallery | 미술관 |
| 09 | get up | 일어나다 |
| 10 | glasses | 안경 |
| 11 | know | 알다 |
| 12 | Korean | 한국어, 한국인 |
| 13 | learn | 배우다 |
| 14 | live | 살다 |
| 15 | math | 수학 |

| | 단어 | 뜻 |
|---|---|---|
| 16 | morning | 아침 |
| 17 | name | 이름 |
| 18 | newspaper | 신문 |
| 19 | night | 밤 |
| 20 | outside | 밖에 |
| 21 | pet | 애완동물 |
| 22 | radio | 라디오 |
| 23 | soccer | 축구 |
| 24 | store | 상점 |
| 25 | today | 오늘 |
| 26 | tooth | 치아 |
| 27 | travel | 여행하다 |
| 28 | traveler | 여행자 |
| 29 | vegetable | 야채 |
| 30 | wear | 입다, 쓰다 |

## 1 다음 우리말 뜻에 해당하는 영어 단어를 쓰세요.

01 여행하다 → travel
02 신문 → ______
03 입다, 쓰다 → ______
04 야구모자 → ______
05 배우다 → ______
06 밤 → ______
07 치아 → ______
08 수학 → ______
09 이름 → ______
10 아침 → ______
11 일어나다 → ______
12 밖에 → ______
13 만화(의) → ______
14 한국어, 한국인 → ______
15 여행자 → ______
16 (값이) ~이다 → ______

## 2 다음 영어 단어에 해당하는 우리말 뜻을 쓰세요.

01 children → 아이들
02 today → ______
03 dollar → ______
04 vegetable → ______
05 soccer → ______
06 cook → ______
07 gallery → ______
08 store → ______
09 radio → ______
10 pet → ______
11 know → ______
12 chat → ______
13 live → ______
14 glasses → ______

# CHAPTER 7

## 1 다음 우리말과 일치하도록 괄호 안에서 알맞은 것을 고르세요.

01 The boy is ( my / your ) friend.
그 소년은 나의 친구다.

02 This is ( my / his ) brother.
이 사람이 그의 오빠다.

03 The student does ( his / their ) homework.
그 학생은 그의 숙제를 한다.

04 Ms. Johnson is ( your / our ) teacher.
존슨 부인은 우리의 선생님이다.

05 Susan brushes ( his / her ) teeth every day.
수잔은 매일 그녀의 이를 닦는다.

06 ( Its / My ) tail is very long.
그것의 꼬리는 매우 길다.

07 I love ( his / him ) very much.
나는 그를 매우 사랑한다.

08 The brothers clean ( his / their ) house.
그 형제들은 그들의 집을 청소한다.

09 My friends miss ( your / you ).
나의 친구들은 너를 그리워한다.

10 We take care of ( his / her ) dog.
우리는 그녀의 개를 돌본다.

11 She visits ( us / his ) every day.
그녀는 매일 우리를 방문한다.

12 I meet ( their / them ) after school.
나는 방과 후에 그들을 만난다.

## 2 다음 우리말과 일치하도록 빈칸에 알맞은 말을 쓰세요.

01 Cindy washes ___her___ face.
신디가 그녀의 얼굴을 닦는다.

02 The woman is __________ teacher.
그 여자는 우리의 선생님이다.

03 It's __________ computer.
그것은 그의 컴퓨터다.

04 __________ bag is on the desk.
나의 가방은 책상 위에 있다.

05 I invite __________ to my birthday party.
나는 그들을 내 생일 파티에 초대한다.

06 They know __________ very well.
그들은 그녀를 매우 잘 안다.

07 She writes in __________ diary every night.
그녀는 매일 밤 그녀의 일기를 쓴다.

08 My dad washes __________ hands before meals.
나의 아빠는 식사 전에 그의 손을 씻는다.

09 They wash __________ car on Sunday.
그들은 일요일에 그들의 자동차를 세차한다.

10 Susan meets __________ every day.
수잔은 그를 매일 만난다.

11 Mr. Thompson teaches __________.
톰슨 씨는 우리를 가르친다.

12 My mom buys __________ at the market.
나의 엄마는 그것을 시장에서 산다.

# CHAPTER 7

## 1 다음 괄호 안에서 알맞은 것을 고르세요.

01 Apples are in the basket. ( He / She / They ) are red.
사과들이 바구니에 있다. 그것들은 빨갛다.

02 A girl is in the park. ( I / He / She ) is tall.
한 소녀가 공원에 있다. 그녀는 키가 크다.

03 My dad works at a bank. ( I / He / She ) is kind.
나의 아빠는 은행에서 일한다. 그는 친절하다.

04 My bag is on the desk. ( It / He / She ) is grey.
나의 가방이 책상 위에 있다. 그것은 회색이다.

05 The children play basketball. ( We / You / They ) are happy.
그 아이들은 농구를 한다. 그들은 행복하다.

06 He has a cat. ( It / He / She ) has green eyes.
그는 고양이가 있다. 그것은 초록 눈을 가지고 있다.

07 Ken is my brother. ( I / He / She ) is ten years old.
켄은 나의 남동생이다. 그는 10살이다.

08 The women are in the shop. ( We / You / They ) are my aunts.
그 여자들은 가게에 있다. 그들은 나의 고모들이다.

09 John and I play the piano. ( We / You / They ) are best friends.
존과 나는 피아노를 친다. 우리는 친한 친구들이다.

10 You and Tom clean the room. ( We / You / They ) are diligent.
너와 톰은 그 방을 청소한다. 너희들은 부지런하다

## 2 다음 우리말과 일치하도록 빈칸에 알맞은 말을 쓰세요.

01 My mom works at a restaurant. ___She___ is a chef.
나의 엄마는 식당에서 일한다. 그녀는 주방장이다.

02 I have a brother. __________ is five years old.
나는 남동생이 있다. 그는 다섯 살이다.

03 The man is in the garage. __________ fixes his car.
그 남자는 차고에 있다. 그는 그의 차를 고친다.

04 John and Tom are my friends. __________ play soccer.
존과 톰은 나의 친구들이다. 그들은 축구를 한다.

05 Jen and I are tall. __________ are basketball players.
젠과 나는 키가 크다. 우리는 농구 선수들이다.

06 The girls are from Vietnam. __________ are singers.
그 소녀들은 베트남에서 왔다. 그들은 가수들이다.

07 His dog is very small. __________ is two weeks old.
그의 개는 아주 작다. 그것은 태어난 지 2주가 되었다.

08 You and Ben read a lot. __________ are smart.
너와 벤은 독서를 많이 한다. 너희들은 영리하다.

09 The printer is on the desk. __________ is broken.
그 프린터는 책상 위에 있다. 그것은 고장 났다.

10 Joanne is an animal doctor. __________ is my aunt.
조앤은 수의사다. 그녀는 나의 고모다.

# REview TEST

**1** 다음 우리말과 일치하도록 밑줄 친 부분을 바르게 고쳐 쓰세요.

01 She washes his face in the morning. → her
그녀는 아침에 그녀의 얼굴을 씻는다.

02 I do me homework after school. → ____________
나는 방과 후에 나의 숙제를 한다.

03 The two girls are him sisters. → ____________
그 두 소녀들은 그의 여동생들이다.

04 My parents love his. → ____________
나의 부모님은 그를 사랑한다.

05 She buys his pants at the market. → ____________
그녀는 시장에서 그녀의 바지를 산다.

06 The boy meets their on Monday. → ____________
그 소년은 월요일에 그들을 만난다.

07 Mr. Kim teaches our. → ____________
김 선생님이 우리를 가르친다.

08 His dog wags it tail back and forth. → ____________
그의 개는 그것의 꼬리를 앞뒤로 흔든다.

09 You parents are very nice. → ____________
너의 부모님들은 무척 좋으시다.

10 We help she every day. → ____________
우리는 매일 그녀를 돕는다.

## 2 다음 우리말과 일치하도록 보기에서 알맞은 말을 골라 문장을 완성하세요.

| She | He | We | They | It | them | us | his |
|---|---|---|---|---|---|---|---|

01 My sister is a musician. ___She___ plays the violin.
나의 누나는 음악가다. 그녀는 바이올린을 연주한다.

02 Three men are on the stage. __________ are dancers.
세 명의 남자들이 무대에 있다. 그들은 무용수들이다.

03 My computer is old. __________ is broken.
내 컴퓨터는 오래됐다. 그것은 고장 났다.

04 My dad washes __________ car on Sunday.
나의 아빠는 일요일에 그의 차를 세차한다.

05 My parents take care of __________.
나의 부모님들이 우리를 돌본다.

06 My brother is a baby. __________ cries at night.
나의 남동생은 아기다. 그는 밤에 운다.

07 Jessie and Jessica are my sisters. I love __________.
제시와 제시카는 내 누나들이다. 나는 그들을 사랑한다.

08 Nick and I go to the mall. __________ need shoes.
닉과 나는 쇼핑몰에 간다. 우리는 신발들이 필요하다.

# Vocabulary TEST

| | 단어 | 뜻 |
|---|---|---|
| 01 | aunt | 고모, 이모 |
| 02 | bag | 가방 |
| 03 | bank | 은행 |
| 04 | basketball | 농구 |
| 05 | before | ~ 전에 |
| 06 | best | 최고의 |
| 07 | birthday | 생일 |
| 08 | broken | 고장 난 |
| 09 | care | 돌봄 |
| 10 | chef | 주방장 |
| 11 | clean | 청소하다 |
| 12 | cry | 울다 |
| 13 | desk | 책상 |
| 14 | face | 얼굴 |
| 15 | friend | 친구 |

| | 단어 | 뜻 |
|---|---|---|
| 16 | grey | 회색(의) |
| 17 | invite | 초대하다 |
| 18 | love | 사랑하다 |
| 19 | mall | 쇼핑몰 |
| 20 | musician | 음악가 |
| 21 | pants | 바지 |
| 22 | parent | 부모 |
| 23 | party | 파티 |
| 24 | piano | 피아노 |
| 25 | printer | 프린터 |
| 26 | tail | 꼬리 |
| 27 | teacher | 선생님 |
| 28 | wag | 흔들다 |
| 29 | wash | 닦다 |
| 30 | week | 일주일 |

# CHAPTER 7

## 1 다음 우리말 뜻에 해당하는 영어 단어를 쓰세요.

01 고장 난 → broken
02 부모 → ________
03 가방 → ________
04 프린터 → ________
05 닦다 → ________
06 친구 → ________
07 회색(의) → ________
08 돌봄 → ________
09 초대하다 → ________
10 사랑하다 → ________
11 최고의 → ________
12 피아노 → ________
13 선생님 → ________
14 은행 → ________
15 고모, 이모 → ________
16 쇼핑몰 → ________

## 2 다음 영어 단어에 해당하는 우리말 뜻을 쓰세요.

01 basketball → 농구
02 week → ________
03 musician → ________
04 before → ________
05 birthday → ________
06 pants → ________
07 tail → ________
08 face → ________
09 clean → ________
10 wag → ________
11 desk → ________
12 cry → ________
13 chef → ________
14 party → ________

# CHAPTER 8

## 1 다음 우리말과 일치하도록 괄호 안에서 알맞은 것을 고르세요.

01 I ( can / can't ) play the harp. 나는 하프를 연주할 수 있다.

02 My sister ( can / can't ) drive a car. 나의 누나는 자동차를 운전할 수 있다.

03 The boy ( can / can't ) read a newspaper. 그 소년은 신문을 읽을 수 없다.

04 The children ( can / can't ) play volleyball. 그 아이들은 배구를 할 수 있다.

05 She can ( dances / dance ) well. 그녀는 춤을 잘 출 수 있다.

06 They can ( swim / swims ) in the pool. 그들은 수영장에서 수영할 수 있다.

07 Josh can ( do / does ) his homework. 조쉬는 그의 숙제를 할 수 있다.

08 ( Does / Can ) you jump high? 당신은 높이 뛸 수 있나요?

09 ( Do / Can ) we talk in class? 수업 중에 우리가 말할 수 있나요?

10 Can they ( gets / get ) up early? 그들은 일찍 일어날 수 있나요?

11 Can you ( call / calls ) me later? 당신은 나중에 나에게 전화할 수 있나요?

12 My mom ( can / do ) make macarons. 나의 엄마는 마카롱을 만들 수 있다.

**2** 다음 우리말과 일치하도록 주어진 단어를 이용하여 빈칸에 알맞은 표현을 쓰세요.

**01** 그는 영어로 말할 수 있다. (speak)

➡ He ___can___ ___speak___ in English.

**02** 그녀는 그 수학 문제를 풀 수 있다. (solve)

➡ She ________ ________ the math problem.

**03** 그 개는 빨리 달릴 수 있다. (run)

➡ The dog ________ ________ fast.

**04** 그 소녀는 매운 음식을 먹을 수 없다. (eat)

➡ The girl ________ ________ spicy food.

**05** 그 학생은 그 질문에 답할 수 있다. (answer)

➡ The student ________ ________ the question.

**06** 그 고양이는 그 높은 나무를 오를 수 있다. (climb)

➡ The cat ________ ________ the tall tree.

**07** 나는 오늘 보고서를 끝낼 수 없다. (finish)

➡ I ________ ________ the report today.

**08** 그 건축가는 다리를 지을 수 있다. (build)

➡ The architect ________ ________ a bridge.

**09** 그 여자는 말을 탈 수 없다. (ride)

➡ The woman ________ ________ a horse.

**10** 나는 지하철로 학교에 갈 수 있다. (go)

➡ I ________ ________ to school by subway.

# CHAPTER 8

## 1 다음 우리말과 일치하도록 괄호 안에서 알맞은 것을 고르세요.

01 I ( am going to / am going ) go shopping tomorrow.
나는 내일 쇼핑하러 갈 것이다.

02 I'm going to ( play / plays ) tennis with my friend.
나는 나의 친구와 테니스를 칠 것이다.

03 They ( is / are ) going to go skating on Sunday.
그들은 일요일에 스케이트를 타러 갈 것이다.

04 We are going to ( visit / visits ) our grandparents.
우리는 우리의 조부모님들을 방문할 것이다.

05 The baby is going to ( is / be ) two years old next year.
그 아기는 내년에 두 살이 될 것이다.

06 ( Are / Be ) you going to read a book?
당신은 책을 읽을 건가요?

07 Is he going to ( study / studies ) science after dinner?
그는 저녁식사 후에 과학을 공부할 건가요?

08 She's ( going / going to ) take a walk.
그녀는 산책을 할 것이다.

09 The boy ( be going to / is going to ) fix his bike.
그 소년은 그의 자전거를 고칠 것이다.

10 My mom is going ( make / to make ) Italian food.
나의 엄마는 이탈리아 요리를 만들 것이다.

## 2 다음 주어진 단어를 이용하여 우리말과 일치하도록 문장을 완성하세요.

01 He ___is going to clean___ his room. (clean)
그는 그의 방을 청소할 것이다.

02 They ______________ a movie tomorrow. (watch)
그들은 내일 영화를 보지 않을 것이다.

03 We ______________ a museum on Saturday. (visit)
우리는 토요일에 박물관을 방문할 것이다.

04 I ______________ at home this weekend. (stay)
나는 이번 주말에 집에 머물 것이다.

05 The brothers ______________. (eat out)
그 형제들은 외식하러 가지 않을 것이다.

06 They ______________ soccer after school. (play)
그들은 방과 후에 축구를 할 것이다.

07 Susan ______________ early tomorrow. (get up)
수잔은 내일 일찍 일어날 것이다.

08 My mom ______________ dinner. (cook)
나의 엄마는 저녁식사를 요리하지 않을 것이다.

09 John ______________ a shower after dinner. (take)
존은 저녁식사 후에 샤워를 할 것이다.

10 We ______________ English together. (study)
우리는 함께 영어를 공부할 것이다.

# REview TEST

**1** 다음 우리말과 일치하도록 주어진 단어를 이용하여 빈칸에 알맞은 표현을 쓰세요.

**01** **A:** 당신의 아빠는 영어로 말할 수 있나요? (speak)
**B:** 예, 할 수 있어요.
**A:** ___Can___ your dad ___speak___ English?
**B:** Yes, ___he___ ___can___.

**02** **A:** 그녀는 그 과학 문제를 풀 수 있나요? (solve)
**B:** 아니요, 할 수 없어요.
**A:** __________ she __________ the science problem?
**B:** No, __________ __________.

**03** **A:** 그 새는 높이 날 수 있나요? (fly)
**B:** 아니요, 할 수 없어요.
**A:** __________ the bird __________ high?
**B:** No, __________ __________.

**04** **A:** 당신들은 바다에서 수영할 수 있나요? (swim)
**B:** 예, 할 수 있어요.
**A:** __________ you __________ in the sea?
**B:** Yes, __________ __________.

**05** **A:** 당신의 언니는 피아노를 칠 수 있나요? (play)
**B:** 예, 할 수 있어요.
**A:** __________ your sister __________ the piano?
**B:** Yes, __________ __________.

**06** **A:** 당신은 그 질문에 답할 수 있나요? (answer)
**B:** 아니요, 할 수 없어요.
**A:** __________ you __________ the question?
**B:** No, __________ __________.

## 2 다음 우리말과 일치하도록 주어진 단어를 이용해서 문장과 부정문을 완성하세요.

**01** 나는 나의 개한테 먹이를 줄 수 있다. (feed)

➡ I ___can feed___ my dog.

➡ **부정문** I ___can't feed___ my dog.

**02** 나는 내일 영화를 보러 갈 것이다. (go)

➡ I ________________ to the movies tomorrow.

➡ **부정문** I ________________ to the movies tomorrow.

**03** 그는 그녀의 생일 파티에 올 수 있다. (come)

➡ He ________________ to her birthday party.

➡ **부정문** He ________________ to her birthday party.

**04** 우리는 저녁식사 후에 산책을 할 것이다. (take)

➡ We ________________ a walk after dinner.

➡ **부정문** We ________________ a walk after dinner.

**05** 너는 그 무거운 상자를 들어 올릴 수 있다. (lift)

➡ You ________________ the heavy box.

➡ **부정문** You ________________ the heavy box.

**06** 그들은 안전벨트를 맬 것이다. (wear)

➡ They ________________ seatbelts.

➡ **부정문** They ________________ seatbelts.

# Vocabulary TEST

| | 단어 | 뜻 |
|---|---|---|
| 01 | answer | 대답(하다) |
| 02 | architect | 건축가 |
| 03 | board | 보드, 판자 |
| 04 | build | 짓다 |
| 05 | call | 전화하다 |
| 06 | climb | 오르다 |
| 07 | dance | 춤추다 |
| 08 | feed | 먹이를 주다 |
| 09 | finish | 마치다 |
| 10 | food | 음식 |
| 11 | grandparent | 조부모 |
| 12 | horse | 말 |
| 13 | lift | 들어 올리다 |
| 14 | movie | 영화 |
| 15 | pool | 수영장 |

| | 단어 | 뜻 |
|---|---|---|
| 16 | question | 질문 |
| 17 | report | 보고서 |
| 18 | ride | 타다 |
| 19 | room | 방 |
| 20 | science | 과학 |
| 21 | sea | 바다 |
| 22 | seatbelt | 안전벨트 |
| 23 | shower | 샤워 |
| 24 | solve | 풀다 |
| 25 | spicy | 매운 |
| 26 | subway | 지하철 |
| 27 | swim | 수영하다 |
| 28 | tomorrow | 내일 |
| 29 | volleyball | 배구 |
| 30 | weekend | 주말 |

## 1 다음 우리말 뜻에 해당하는 영어 단어를 쓰세요.

| | | | | | |
|---|---|---|---|---|---|
| 01 | 안전벨트 | → seatbelt | 02 | 오르다 | → ________ |
| 03 | 짓다 | → ________ | 04 | 춤추다 | → ________ |
| 05 | 보드, 판자 | → ________ | 06 | 건축가 | → ________ |
| 07 | 먹이를 주다 | → ________ | 08 | 지하철 | → ________ |
| 09 | 방 | → ________ | 10 | 말 | → ________ |
| 11 | 영화 | → ________ | 12 | 주말 | → ________ |
| 13 | 들어 올리다 | → ________ | 14 | 풀다 | → ________ |
| 15 | 매운 | → ________ | 16 | 조부모 | → ________ |

## 2 다음 영어 단어에 해당하는 우리말 뜻을 쓰세요.

| | | | | | |
|---|---|---|---|---|---|
| 01 | ride | → 타다 | 02 | volleyball | → ________ |
| 03 | shower | → ________ | 04 | finish | → ________ |
| 05 | report | → ________ | 06 | tomorrow | → ________ |
| 07 | food | → ________ | 08 | question | → ________ |
| 09 | science | → ________ | 10 | answer | → ________ |
| 11 | sea | → ________ | 12 | pool | → ________ |
| 13 | call | → ________ | 14 | swim | → ________ |

# Memo

# Memo

# Memo

GRAMMAR MENTOR JOY

WORK BOOK

nkbooks
www.inkbooks.co.kr
무료 학습자료 다운로드 | 구매문의 02) 455 9620